We're Hungry!

Batch Cooking Your Family Will Love

We're Hungry!

CIARA ATTWELL

For Chickpea and Buddy

CONTENTS

INTRODUCTION

For seven years now, I've shared my journey online from reluctant to a more enthusiastic home cook. I've documented the early years of feeding struggles with my children, from the overwhelming weaning stage through to the fussy toddler years, sharing the recipes, tips and tricks that have worked for me. My kids are now ten and seven, and, although I still deal with picky-eaters on a daily basis (one day they will eat broccoli for me!), the way in which I cook and we eat as a family has changed somewhat in the past couple of years.

Like most families, our day-to-day life is pretty hectic with school runs, clubs and playdates for the kids and busy work schedules for myself and my husband. Whilst I love nothing more than pottering around the kitchen creating new recipes, the reality is that most family meals are thrown together in haste without a whole lot of planning or preparation.

Meal planning is fantastic. It can do so much to help alleviate the stress of shopping and cooking and cut down on food waste. But, personally, I find it difficult to plan more than a couple of days in advance and a lot of my online followers have said the same. No two weeks are the same in our house and plans regularly change from day to day.

I needed a system for cooking that was simple but easily adaptable, that could alleviate some of the weekday meal panic but not require me to spend hours in the kitchen on a Sunday prepping food for the week. I knew batch cooking was the key but I also knew that it needed to be more than

just cooking double of everything, chucking it in the freezer and hoping that one day you remember to defrost it!

The aim of this book is to redefine batch cooking for the modern family, giving you recipes that can be matched to your most busy and least busy days. The kitchen equipment has been pared back to a minimum and all ingredients can be easily found at a local shop or supermarket. There are no complicated cooking instructions or methods. Simple family meals made fuss-free is the key. This book is going to save you time, money and stress and I can't wait for you to get started!

ABOUT THIS BOOK

This book contains 100 recipes broken down into nine chapters. Along with chapters for Breakfast, Lunch and Stock, Sides & Sauces, there are five chapters devoted to family meals. Each recipe will tell you roughly how long you will need to spend prepping and cooking along with a list of the equipment that you will need. There will also be a detailed explanation of how each recipe can be batch-cooked, along with specific instructions for refrigerating, freezing and defrosting.

BREAKFAST

Breakfast is usually the least-thought-out meal of the day, but these simple and easy recipes will give you options other than cereal or toast to reach for on busy mornings. Whether you have young children at home or teenagers who need a grab-and-go breakfast, I have recipes to suit the whole family.

LUNCH

Whether you are looking for ideas for lunch at home or foods that can be packed up for school or the office, these recipes will help to liven up your midday meal and give you something to look forward to other than a boring sandwich!

ONE-POT WONDERS

These are my ultimate 5pm panic meals. Days when you have nothing planned or prepared but you need to get dinner on the table fast! All of these recipes can be cooked on the hob in around thirty minutes using just one saucepan or pot. Minimum stress, minimum washing up, but maximum taste and satisfaction! My one-pot meals make ideal leftovers for the fridge. Whether you save a portion or cook extra, pop the leftovers into the fridge for lunch or dinner within the next couple of days.

FAMILY FAVOURITES

This chapter contains classic family-friendly meals that might take a bit more time to cook but are ideal to make in batches and freeze for another day. If you're going to make the effort to cook foods like chicken goujons, vegetable pies and meatballs from scratch, then it really is worth adding just a few extra minutes to your prep and making a double batch.

SLOW COOKER

I took a poll of my followers online last year and over eighty per cent said they owned and used a slow cooker, which I was so pleased about. I absolutely love my slow cooker and it has played a vital part in my fuss-free approach to family meals. All of these recipes can be prepped in just a few minutes in the morning, leaving you to get on with work, school runs and the general day-to-day chaos of family life. If you don't already own a slow cooker then I would one hundred per cent recommend getting one and I give a bit more advice about this on page 15.

COOK ONCE, EAT TWICE

Leftovers are fantastic for an instant meal the next day, but I know that not everyone wants to eat the same dinner two days in a row. So my 'Cook Once, Eat Twice' chapter shows you how you can turn your leftovers into a brand-new tasty meal the next day with just a couple of new ingredients and a few minutes extra prep.

FREEZER STASH BAGS

My Freezer Stash Bags will make you feel like a food prep master. These are bags of ingredients prepped and filled ahead of time and frozen. On busy days they just need to be defrosted and either popped into the slow cooker in the morning or cooked in the oven or on the hob later that evening.

STOCK, SIDES & SAUCES

This chapter contains my favourite basic stocks, sides and sauces that I always have to hand to complement or complete a family meal on busy days.

BIG BATCH SNACKS

In my opinion, no family cookbook is complete without a substantial chapter on snacks! As parents, most of us are probably asked for a snack at least three times a day and the cost of shop-bought snacks soon adds up. Finding a balance between 'treats' for the kids and healthy, filling ingredients can be difficult. Most of my snacks are relatively low in sugar but still kid-friendly. Most are also freezable and lots are suitable for lunch boxes too.

HOW TO USE THIS BOOK

Included in each recipe are the above icons to show allergy information. However, all recipes are easily adaptable to make them more allergy-friendly. All flour and pasta can be substituted for gluten-free versions and milk and butter for dairy-free alternatives. Dairy-free cheese can also be used, but just be aware that it doesn't always resemble normal cheese in that it doesn't brown or become stringy. Substitute stock cubes, soy sauce etc. for gluten- and dairy-free alternatives. Note some shop-bought pastas may also contain egg. There is also veggie Parmesan widely available for using in the recipes too.

INGREDIENT INFO
Unless specifically stated, all oil can be olive oil, rapeseed oil or vegetable oil.

Butter and coconut oil can be used inter-changeably in the Snacks chapter. Butter is always unsalted.

All eggs are medium.

SEASONING
Salt and pepper are optional in all recipes. Except for a few recipes I haven't used any salt or pepper in an attempt to keep them as kid-friendly as possible. Feel free to add some seasoning before or after cooking if you like.

PORTION SIZES
Most recipes are designed with a family of four in mind. If a recipe feeds four then it will be just enough for two adults and two children. If your children are very young or older teenagers then you may want to adjust the quantities accordingly.

INGREDIENT HACKS

Over the past couple of years I've learned that home cooking doesn't have to mean that absolutely every ingredient has been prepped, chopped and cooked by you. Feeding a family several times a day is no easy task and I have no shame in admitting that I use a lot of shortcuts and cheat ingredients to make my life a little easier in the kitchen. Here are some of my favourite ones.

FROZEN ONIONS & GARLIC

These are my ultimate time-savers. I very rarely chop onions or garlic anymore. It's just too easy to pull them straight from the freezer and add them into the pan or slow cooker. I buy mine from the supermarket but you could also peel, chop and freeze your own.

When a recipe requires one onion use the equivalent amount of chopped frozen onion. It doesn't matter if it's a bit more or less. The same with garlic. Most of my recipes state 'crushed' garlic, but finely chopped frozen garlic is perfect too.

Frozen chopped ginger is another ingredient that I always have in my freezer and it prevents the waste that often comes with buying fresh ginger.

FROZEN VEG

You will always find a bag of chopped mixed frozen vegetables in my freezer. They're brilliant to add to simple meals like pasta to bulk it out and add some nutrients. Frozen veg is usually cheaper than fresh and, of course,

doesn't go off quickly, so it's a great way to cut down on food waste and save you money.

As well as mixed vegetables, I also keep a bag of peas and sweetcorn in my freezer too, either to add to recipes or to serve up on the side.

Several of the recipes in this book use frozen diced cauliflower. On page 161 I show you how to make your own, but you can also buy packs of ready-diced frozen cauliflower too.

HERBS

I love fresh herbs. You really can't beat the aroma of fresh basil or rosemary. But for this book I decided to use mainly dried herbs as they are cheap, accessible and easy to store.

If you would prefer to use fresh or frozen herbs that's totally fine. You can buy packets of chopped frozen herbs which are brilliant too.

MICROWAVE RICE

I always have a few packs of plain boiled rice and vegetable rice in my cupboard. Cooking a pan of rice on the hob isn't difficult, but when you need to get a meal on the table fast then you can't beat the convenience of microwave rice.

CHILLI SAUCE

I love a kick to my food but to keep my recipes kid-friendly I never use more than a mild curry powder or paste. Instead I have an array of chilli sauces that I use to spice up dishes. A lemon or herb chilli sauce is great for chicken or fish. A BBQ chilli sauce adds a lovely deep smoky flavour to tomato-based recipes like bolognese or chilli. And a classic hot sauce can be used on pretty much everything and anything!

CURRY PASTES

As well as curry powder, I use curry pastes in a few recipes. I always have one Indian-style curry paste as well as one Thai curry paste in the cupboard. They add bags of instant flavour to recipes, especially dishes that need to be cooked quickly.

PUFF PASTRY

I very rarely make my own pastry. If the shop-bought product is amazing then why spend hours in the kitchen trying to perfect it! I always buy the ready-rolled version as it's super easy to use and the quantity is perfect for my recipe servings. A roll tends to keep in the fridge for a couple of weeks when bought but can also be frozen and defrosted.

DRIED BREADCRUMBS

Fresh breadcrumbs are great but, personally, I prefer to use the dried version. I find that they give a finer coating to recipes like nuggets and don't burn as easily when cooking. In this book I use both normal dried breadcrumbs and panko breadcrumbs. Panko breadcrumbs are a Japanese-style breadcrumb, a little coarser than normal dried breadcrumbs but they give a really crispy finish. Both type of breadcrumbs will keep for months so are a great store cupboard staple.

BATCH COOKING ESSENTIALS

In this book I wanted to pare back the equipment needed to make my recipes. I love a kitchen gadget but I appreciate that most people don't want their precious kitchen space over-run with appliances and utensils that they only use a few times a year.

Here are my batch cooking essentials.

SLOW COOKER

I have dedicated a whole section of this cookbook to slow cooker recipes, such is my love for the slow cooker! But listen up … you do not have to spend a lot of money on one. The more expensive options have timers etc., but I use a £13 supermarket slow cooker and it's one of my most-loved kitchen gadgets.

BLENDER & FOOD PROCESSOR

Most recipes that require blending can be done with a stand blender or a stick blender. Stick blenders are much cheaper and, of course, take up a lot less room. The only recipes where you will need a stand blender (or a smoothie maker) are the Smoothie Bags (see page 38) and the Pesto recipes (see pages 154-155). The rest can be done with a stick blender.

There are a few recipes that require a food processor, but I have tried to keep these to a minimum. If, however, you do wish to buy a food processor then there are a lot of great budget options available now.

SHALLOW CASSEROLE DISH

Probably my second-favourite piece of kitchen equipment is a shallow casserole dish. I use it for all my One-Pot Wonder recipes along with a lot of other recipes cooked on the hob or in the oven. Again, you don't have to spend a lot of money. Basic cast-iron casserole dishes start from about £30 online and will last you years.

SAUCEPANS & FRYING PAN

A simple set of saucepans will do so many dishes, along with a decent-sized frying pan. Non-stick is essential in my book, but, again, you can shop around for deals online.

ROASTING TINS & TRAYS

A couple of cookie-sheet-style baking trays are essential and also one large deeper tin for roasts.

BAKING DISHES & LOAF TIN

Some smaller glass or ceramic baking dishes or Pyrex dishes are also needed but are completely versatile. I use mine for both savoury meals and also for snacks that have to be baked.

A loaf tin is necessary for banana bread recipes.

FREEZER BAGS & CONTAINERS

These are absolutely essential for batch cooking. You can use plastic freezer bags that you can buy in the supermarket. Remember that they are reusable so don't throw them away after one use. Wash them in warm soapy water and dry well. You can also buy more durable plastic or silicone food bags online.

You will also need some glass or plastic containers for freezing. Keep the plastic containers from takeaways. These are brilliant and the perfect size for storing single portions. Glass containers with plastic lids are also great and will last a long time if you take care of them.

GLASS JARS & JUGS

A few big glass jars are great to store my Granola Bark (see page 31) and Big Batch Brownie Mix (see page 180) recipes. Having see-through jars rather than tins or containers means I'm more likely to be reminded to use the food!

One small and one large glass jug are ideal for measuring stock and melting ingredients in the microwave.

FREEZING TRAY OR PLATE

You will see that in lots of recipes I recommend 'flash-freezing' foods. This stops foods like chicken goujons, muffins and cookies from sticking together when frozen. I have a specific plastic tray that I use as my freezing tray. I know it fits perfectly into my freezer and I would recommend you have a look in your kitchen for something similar.

SHARPIE PENS & STICKERS

Labelling your freezer food is important. You want to be able to tell instantly what it is and when it needs to be used by. You can use marker pens like a Sharpie to write directly onto bags or stickers are another great option too.

SILICONE MUFFIN CASES

Silicone muffin cases are a great alternative to paper cases. They are obviously reusable, but they are also completely non-stick making them ideal for 'healthier' muffins that don't have a high fat content and are more likely to stick to paper cases.

I also use them as little inserts in the kids' lunch box. They are perfect for holding berries and chopped veg or for keeping foods separated from each other.

PARCHMENT PAPER / SILICONE BAKING SHEET

I always line baking trays just to keep the washing up to a minimum. You can also use silicone baking sheets. You can buy them online for just a few pounds and they're a fantastic reusable alternative.

TIPS & BEST PRACTICES FOR BATCH COOKING

Whilst writing this book I spoke with some people about their reluctance to batch cook and the number one reason for not doing it seemed to be a fear of doing it wrong and a worry about food safety. But follow my basic guidelines below and you'll have nothing to worry about. In no time you'll be batching, freezing and defrosting like a pro!

COOL FOOD & QUICKLY

Cooked food must always be cooled down before it is put into the fridge or freezer. Very big pots of food can take some time to cool so transfer into smaller bowls or containers to help speed up the process.

CHOOSE THE RIGHT STORAGE

Most people don't have unlimited space in their fridge or freezer, so make sure to choose the right storage for your food. For example, if you have a small portion of casserole to freeze, do not put it in a large container! The excess air in the container will cause freezer burn and, of course, it will also be a waste of space. Use a small container or a freezer bag instead. Always push the air out of the freezer bags before sealing.

Similarly, don't overfill containers or bags. Leave a little room for the food to expand when it is frozen.

THINK ABOUT PORTIONS

When batch cooking family meals, consider how they are going to be used when defrosted. If you always eat meals together as a family then it's fine to freeze a large portion. But, for example, if you have an older child who gets home late a few times a week from school or clubs you may want some single portions in your freezer too.

FLASH FREEZING

You will see me mention flash freezing in several recipes. Do not skip this step! It will prevent foods like chicken goujons, muffins and cookies from sticking together when frozen. I use a specific tray or plate for this (see previous page). It will take a maximum of 1 hour for the foods to get hard and they can then be transferred into freezer bags or containers.

LABELLING

Labelling is key to avoiding food waste. There's no point spending time and money on batch cooking if you can't identify what's in your freezer. Use a Sharpie to write directly onto bags. Stickers are great when reusing bags and containers.

DEFROSTING

Defrosting food safely is very important, but it doesn't have to be complicated. As a rule I always defrost meals in the fridge overnight. It's the safest way to defrost cooked food especially if it contains meat. Place the freezer bag or container in a bowl to catch any excess moisture that comes off.

With small batches of sauces like my Everyday Tomato Sauce and No-Cook Pestos (see pages 153-155), I sometimes defrost at room temperature or by gently heating in a saucepan if I am in a rush.

I rarely defrost large batches of food in the microwave as the result can be a bit uneven, resulting in some food being overcooked and other parts still frozen. If you do want to use the microwave, do it in short bursts and stop to stir the food often.

Snacks like muffins, cookies and energy bites can be popped into a lunch box and defrosted in a couple of hours.

COOKING FROM FROZEN

Some of the recipes can be cooked directly from frozen which saves the hassle of defrosting. Timings can fluctuate depending on the size and depth of the dish that you are using, so ensure the food is piping hot throughout before serving.

As a rule, you should never cook meat from frozen in the slow cooker as the temperature will not get high enough for long enough to cook the meat safely. Therefore the only slow cooker recipe which can be cooked from frozen is Chunky Vegetable Soup on page 148.

REHEATING

Most cooked foods can be reheated in the microwave or on the hob. Times will depend on the quantity and type of food, but it is always best to do it slowly on a lower temperature, stirring regularly. Ensure food is piping hot throughout before serving.

A QUICK GUIDE TO FOOD STORAGE TIMES

I have set out a very rough guide to storing food at room temperature, in the fridge and in the freezer. Although most foods can be frozen for 2–3 months, I try not to freeze anything for longer than a month. The food will still be of optimum quality after a month and also it forces me to actually use it, and not just leave it to linger in there for months or even years!

My tip would be to have a monthly stocktake of your freezer and plan to use up any meals or snacks that have been in there for at least 3 weeks. This will also help you to plan forward and you'll know how much space you have and what recipes would be best to batch cook in the coming weeks.

FOOD	ROOM TEMPERATURE	FRIDGE	FREEZER
Sweet baked goods like cookies, muffins, etc.	2 Days	2–3 Days	3 Months
Pancakes, fritters, savoury muffins	N/A	2–3 Days	3 Months
Pastries	N/A	2 Days	3 Months
Soup, stews, casseroles, sauces	N/A	2 Days	2 Months
Goujons, nuggets and breaded foods	N/A	2 Days	2 Months
Burgers, meatballs	N/A	2 Days	2 Months
Pasta, risotto	N/A	2 Days	2 Months
Curries, bolognese and chillis	N/A	2 Days	2 Months

BREAKFAST

Baked French Toast Sticks
Chia Berry Breakfast Tarts
Fruity Pancake Bites
Peanut Butter Banana Bread
Ham & Egg Cups
Apple & Pear Rice Pudding
Strawberry Granola
Granola Bark
Coconut Oat Pancakes
Savoury Sheet Pancakes
Power Porridge Pots
Breakfast Fruit Coulis
Berry Porridge Bars
Smoothie Bags

BAKED FRENCH TOAST STICKS

| Makes: 24 | Prep time: 10 minutes | Cook time: 22 minutes | Equipment: Large baking trays |

Batch cooking French toast is easy with my oven-baked method. It makes it super simple to cook several portions at a time and freeze for busy mornings.

INGREDIENTS

8 slices thick wholemeal bread

4 eggs

150ml milk

2 tsp vanilla extract

2 tsp sugar

½ tsp cinnamon

Maple syrup, yoghurt and fruit, to serve

STORING

These French Toast Sticks are best eaten the same day that they are made or else frozen.

FREEZING

Place the sticks on a tray or plate and flash freeze for an hour until hard. Transfer to a freezer bag, push out the air and seal. Freeze for up to 2 months.

Reheat directly from frozen by placing the sticks in the toaster on the lowest setting for about 3 minutes.

Or defrost at room temperature for 2–2.5 hours or in the microwave for 1.5 minutes.

METHOD

1. Preheat the oven to 200°C/180°C Fan/ Gas Mark 6 and line 2 baking trays with parchment paper.

2. Cut each slice of bread into three.

3. Into a shallow bowl add the eggs, milk and vanilla and mix well.

4. Take a piece of the sliced bread, dip both sides in the egg mixture and then place onto one of the trays. Repeat with all the slices of bread.

5. Mix the sugar and cinnamon together in a small bowl and then sprinkle half of this onto the top of the bread sticks.

6. Bake in the oven for 12 minutes, turn each stick and sprinkle with the remaining sugar. Then bake for a further 10 minutes until golden.

7. Serve 3 sticks per portion topped with maple syrup and a portion of yoghurt and fruit on the side.

CHIA BERRY BREAKFAST TARTS

| Makes: 12 | Prep time: 12 minutes | Cook time: 17 minutes | Equipment: Baking trays and large jug |

You can't beat a hot pastry straight from the oven on a Sunday morning. These delicious breakfast tarts are bursting with berries and energy-boosting chia seeds. And you'll have loads leftover to freeze for another day.

INGREDIENTS

200g frozen mixed berries

1 tbsp chia seeds

2 tsp honey

1 tsp vanilla extract

1 sheet ready-rolled puff pastry

125g cream cheese

yoghurt and fruit, to serve

STORING

These breakfast tarts are best eaten on the day they are made but they can be kept in the fridge for up to 2 days.

FREEZING

Freeze these tarts before cooking. After completing Step 7, place the uncooked parcels onto a tray or plate ensuring that they are not touching. Freeze for a couple of hours until solid then transfer to a freezer bag or container for up to 2 months.

Bake directly from frozen at 200°C/180°C Fan/Gas Mark 6. Place on a lined baking tray and cook for 20–22 minutes.

METHOD

1. Preheat the oven to 200°C/180°C Fan/Gas Mark 6 and line 2 baking trays with parchment paper.

2. Add the frozen berries to a large jug and cook in the microwave for 2–3 minutes until they are soft enough to mash with a fork.

3. Add the chia seeds, honey and vanilla and mix well.

4. Unroll the pastry and cut it into 12 squares, placing six on each tray well-spaced apart.

5. Add a small spoon of cream cheese to the centre of each of the pastry squares.

6. Then add a large spoon of the berry mixture on top.

7. Close the parcel by folding each corner of the pastry into the middle to meet.

8. Bake in the oven for 17 minutes until golden.

9. Serve with some yoghurt and fresh fruit.

FRUITY PANCAKE BITES

| Makes: 12 | Prep time: 7 minutes | Cook time: 22 minutes | Equipment: Muffin tray, large mixing bowl and large jug |

All the great taste of pancakes but in easy-to-make and bite-sized portions.
Ideal for freezing for busy mid-week mornings.

INGREDIENTS

2 tbsp butter, plus extra for greasing (or oil)

300g plain flour

1 tsp baking powder

300ml milk

1 tbsp honey

2 eggs

175g fruit – berries (fresh or frozen), sliced bananas, etc.

STORING

These pancake bites will keep in the fridge for 3 days. They can be eaten cold or reheated in the microwave.

FREEZING

Place the bites on a tray or plate and flash freeze for 1 hour until hard. Transfer to a freezer bag or container and freeze for up to 3 months.

Defrost at room temperature for 2–2.5 hours or in the microwave for 1.5 minutes.

METHOD

1. Preheat the oven to 200°C/180°C Fan/ Gas Mark 6 and grease a 12-hole muffin tray with butter or oil.

2. Add the flour and baking powder to a large bowl and mix with a spoon.

3. Add the butter to a large jug and melt in the microwave.

4. Add the milk, honey and eggs to the melted butter and mix well.

5. Pour this into the bowl with the flour and mix just enough until all the ingredients are well combined.

6. Fill the muffin tray holes with the mixture and add a little fruit on top.

7. Bake in the oven for 20–22 minutes.

8. Allow the pancake bites to cool a little in the tin before removing.

PEANUT BUTTER BANANA BREAD

Packed with nutritious and filling ingredients, this banana bread is ideal to have on hand for a tasty breakfast. You can eat it on its own or spread with peanut butter or jam.

INGREDIENTS

200g plain flour

75g oats

1 tsp baking powder

¾ tsp bicarbonate of soda

75g coconut oil or butter

2 bananas, mashed

150g peanut butter

35g honey

1 egg

75ml milk

STORING

This loaf can be kept in an airtight container for up to 2 days.

FREEZING

To freeze, cut the loaf into slices and wrap individually in plastic wrap or foil. Place all the wrapped slices into a freezer bag or container and freeze for up to 3 months.

The slices will defrost at room temperature in 3 hours.

METHOD

1. Preheat the oven to 200°C/180°C Fan/ Gas Mark 6 and line a 900g (2lb) loaf tin with parchment paper.

2. Add the flour, oats, baking powder and bicarbonate of soda to a large bowl and mix.

3. Add the coconut oil or butter to a large jug and melt in the microwave.

4. To the oil or butter add the mashed bananas, peanut butter, honey, egg and milk and stir.

5. Pour this mixture into the dry ingredients and mix until all the ingredients are well combined.

6. Transfer the mixture into the loaf tin and then bake in the oven for 30 minutes.

7. Cover the top of the tin loosely with foil to prevent the top from over-browning then return to the oven for another 15 minutes.

8. Leave the loaf to cool completely on a wire rack before cutting into 12 slices.

HAM & EGG CUPS

| Makes: 12 | Prep time: 7 minutes | Cook time: 15 minutes | Equipment: Muffin tin |

These fun baked eggs wrapped in ham make a tasty portable breakfast.
Perfect to keep in the fridge for a few days and great for snacks too.

INGREDIENTS

2 tsp oil, for greasing

24 slices of thin or wafer ham or
12 slices of thicker ham

12 eggs

salt and pepper to taste

chopped parsley (optional)

STORING

These Ham & Egg Cups will keep
in an airtight container in the
fridge for 2 days. They can be
eaten cold or reheated in the
microwave.

DIRECTIONS

1. Preheat the oven to 220°C/200°C Fan/
   Gas Mark 7.

2. Use the oil to grease the holes of a 12-hole
   muffin tin.

3. Line each of the holes with two slices of ham (or
   just one if it's thicker cut).

4. Crack an egg in each hole and season the top
   with salt and pepper.

5. Bake in the oven for 15 minutes until golden.

6. Remove and leave to cool for a few minutes in the
   tin to ensure the eggs have set.

7. Sprinkle with a little chopped parsley.

APPLE & PEAR RICE PUDDING

| Serves: 5 | Prep time: 5 minutes | Cook time: 25 minutes | Equipment: Large saucepan |

Rice pudding isn't just a great dessert. Combined with some fruit it makes a really tasty and filling breakfast the kids will love.

INGREDIENTS

1 apple

1 pear

200g pudding rice

1 litre milk (dairy or non-dairy)

1 tbsp chia seeds

1 tsp vanilla extract

STORING

This rice pudding can be kept in a container in the fridge for up to 2 days and reheated on the hob or in the microwave.

FREEZING

Transfer the rice pudding into containers and freeze for up to 3 months.

Defrost in the fridge overnight and reheat on the hob or in the microwave.

METHOD

1. Grate or chop the apple and pear into small pieces. The skin can be left on.

2. Add the fruit to a large saucepan along with the other ingredients.

3. Simmer on low for 25–30 minutes until the rice is cooked.

4. If the rice is still a little undercooked, add some milk and cook for a few extra minutes.

5. Serve with fruit coulis (see page 36) or some jam.

STRAWBERRY GRANOLA

| Serves: 10 | Prep time: 5 minutes | Cook time: 30 minutes | Equipment: Baking trays, large mixing bowl and large jug |

Freeze-dried strawberries add a tasty new flavour to homemade granola. You can buy them in large bags online and the bag will keep fresh for a few months.

INGREDIENTS

250g oats

150g mixed nuts, chopped

30g mixed seeds

4 tbsp oil (coconut oil, light olive oil, etc.)

4 tbsp honey

1 tsp vanilla extract

20g freeze-dried strawberries

STORING

This granola will keep in an airtight jar or container for 2 weeks.

METHOD

1. Preheat the oven to 200°C/180°C Fan/ Gas Mark 6 and line 2 baking trays with parchment paper.

2. Add the oats, chopped nuts and seeds to a large bowl and mix with a spoon.

3. To a jug or glass add the oil, honey and vanilla extract and mix.

4. Pour this into the oat mixture and quickly stir until all the ingredients are well combined.

5. Divide the mixture between the 2 baking trays and bake in the oven for 30 minutes, stirring twice during this time.

6. Remove the trays from the oven and leave the granola to cool and crisp up. Once cooled, add the freeze-dried strawberries.

7. Transfer to an airtight jar or container.

Photograph of Strawberry Granola and Granola Bark can be found on page 20.

GRANOLA BARK

All the taste and nutritional value of homemade granola but in a portable bark or bar, ideal for teenagers who rush out the door in the morning without breakfast.

INGREDIENTS

1 egg

100g honey

50g brown sugar

60g coconut oil or butter

1 tsp vanilla

100ml water

300g oats

120g nuts, chopped

50g wholewheat flour

40g desiccated coconut

30g mixed seeds

yoghurt and berries, to serve

STORING

Store the granola bark in an airtight jar or container for up to 2 weeks.

METHOD

1. Preheat the oven to 200°C/180°C Fan/ Gas Mark 6 and line a large baking tray with parchment paper.

2. Separate the egg white from the yolk and whisk the white until it becomes frothy.

3. Put the honey, brown sugar, coconut oil or butter, vanilla and water into a jug and melt in the microwave.

4. Allow to cool before adding in the whisked egg white.

5. Tip the oats, nuts, wholewheat flour, coconut and seeds into a large bowl and mix.

6. Pour in the wet ingredients and mix well.

7. Transfer the mixture into the baking tray and press down firmly with the back of a spoon to make it as compact as possible.

8. Bake in the oven for 35 minutes until dark brown but not burnt.

9. Leave the granola to cool completely in the tin. It will still be soft at this stage but it will crisp up as it cools.

10. Once completely cool, break the granola into chunks. Serve on its own as a grab-and-go breakfast or broken up over yoghurt and berries.

COCONUT OAT PANCAKES

| Makes: 8 | Prep time: 5 minutes | Cook time: 12 minutes | Equipment: Large mixing bowl and frying pan |

For kids who like traditional pancakes, these coconut oat versions are packed full of healthy ingredients but easy to freeze for an instant mid-week breakfast.

INGREDIENTS

1 banana

2 eggs

200ml tinned coconut milk

1 tbsp honey

150g oats

100g plain flour

½ tsp bicarbonate of soda

2 tbsp desiccated coconut

1 tbsp coconut oil or butter

STORING

These pancakes will keep in the fridge for up to 2 days and can be reheated in the oven or microwave.

FREEZING

To freeze, wrap the pancakes individually or in twos in plastic wrap or foil. Place all the wrapped pancakes into a freezer bag or container and freeze for up to 3 months.

The pancakes will defrost at room temperature in 2 hours or in the microwave for 1-1.5 minutes.

METHOD

1. Mash the banana and add it to a large bowl.

2. Add in the eggs, coconut milk and honey and mix.

3. Add the oats, flour, bicarbonate of soda and desiccated coconut and mix a final time.

4. Heat the oil or butter in a frying pan and add a couple of spoonfuls of the mixture at a time to make each pancake. You should be able to fit 4 pancakes in the pan.

5. Cook for about 3 minutes, flip and cook for another 2-3 minutes on the other side.

6. Remove the pancakes and repeat with the remaining mixture.

SAVOURY SHEET PANCAKES

| Makes: 12 | Prep Time: 4 minutes | Cook time: 15 minutes | Equipment: Baking tray and large mixing bowl |

Did you know that you can bake pancakes? It's a really simple way of cooking a large batch and this savoury version makes for a nice twist on a classic breakfast pancake.

INGREDIENTS

150g plain flour

1 tsp baking powder

½ tsp bicarbonate of soda

200ml milk

2 eggs

2 tsp French mustard

100g grated cheese

50g ham, chopped

30g baby spinach, chopped

½ red pepper, chopped

METHOD

1. Preheat the oven to 200°C/180°C Fan/ Gas Mark 6 and line a shallow baking tray with parchment paper.

2. Add the flour, baking powder and bicarbonate of soda to a large bowl and mix with a spoon.

3. Add the milk and eggs and mix again.

4. Finally add the mustard, cheese, ham, spinach and pepper and mix one last time.

5. Transfer the mixture into the lined baking tray and bake in the oven for 15 minutes.

6. Allow the pancakes to cool a little before cutting into 12 squares.

STORING

These pancakes will keep in the fridge for up to 2 days and can be reheated in the oven or microwave.

FREEZING

To freeze, wrap the pancakes individually or in twos in plastic wrap or foil. Place all the wrapped slices into a freezer bag or container and freeze for up to 3 months.

The slices will defrost at room temperature in 2 hours and can be reheated in the oven or microwave.

POWER PORRIDGE POTS

| Portions: 10 | Prep time: 3 minutes | Cook time: 4 minutes | Equipment: Food processor, large jar and small jars or pots |

Oats are one of the cheapest ingredients you can buy. Rather than pay over the odds for those instant porridge pots, you can easily make your own at home. My recipes contains nuts and seeds for an added nutritional boost.

INGREDIENTS

For the big batch:

500g oats

75g nuts

50g mixed seeds

For each portion:

150ml boiling water

50ml milk (dairy or non-dairy)

1 tsp honey

STORING

The dry porridge mixture will keep in an airtight container for up to 1 month.

METHOD

1. Blitz the oats, nuts and seeds in a food processor until it reaches a flour-like consistency.

2. Transfer into one large airtight jar.

TO MAKE IN A BOWL AT HOME

3. When ready to make, add 60g of the porridge mixture to a bowl.

4. Pour in 150ml of boiling water and mix well.

5. Cover with a plate and leave for 4 minutes.

6. At this stage the porridge will be very thick. Add the milk and honey and stir again.

TO MAKE IN A JAR AT WORK

3. To make in a jar add 60g of the porridge mixture to a small jar with a lid.

4. Add 150ml boiling water straight in, close the lid tightly and shake well.

5. Leave for 4 minutes before adding the milk and honey and mixing with a spoon.

BREAKFAST FRUIT COULIS

| Portions: 10 | Prep time: 1 minute | Cook time: 10 minutes | Equipment: Large saucepan and glass jar or containers |

Frozen fruit is cheap, healthy and so versatile. Turn bags of frozen berries or cherries into a delicious fruit coulis, perfect for adding to yoghurt, porridge or smoothies.

INGREDIENTS

500g frozen fruit

juice of 1 clementine

1 tbsp chia seeds

STORING

This coulis will keep in an airtight jar or container in the fridge for 4 days.

FREEZING

Freeze in small batches in freezer bags or containers for up to 2 months. Defrost at room temperature for 1 hour or overnight in the fridge.

If you freeze in very small batches like ice cube trays you can add these straight from frozen to hot porridge.

METHOD

1. Add the frozen fruit and clementine juice to a saucepan and cook on low for 5–10 minutes until the berries have softened.

2. Remove from the heat and stir in the chia seeds.

3. Leave the mixture to cool then transfer to a jar or a few small containers.

4. Serve on top of yoghurt, with porridge or add to smoothies.

BERRY PORRIDGE BARS

| Makes: 9 | Prep time: 5 minutes | Cook time: 40 minutes | Equipment: Large mixing bowl and baking dish |

These bars are a great alternative for children who don't like porridge. They contain all the nutritional benefits of oats but in a kid-friendly bar form!

INGREDIENTS

250g oats

1 tsp baking powder

400ml milk

1 egg

1 banana, mashed, or 120g apple sauce

3 tbsp honey

1 tsp vanilla

100g frozen mixed berries

STORING

These porridge bars will keep in the fridge for up to 3 days and can be reheated in the oven or microwave.

FREEZING

Place the bars on a tray and flash freeze for 1 hour until hard. Transfer to a freezer bag or container and freeze for up to 3 months. These bars can be eaten cold or reheated in the microwave.

Defrost at room temperature for 3–4 hours. Eat cold or reheat in the microwave.

METHOD

1. Preheat the oven to 200°C/180°C Fan/ Gas Mark 6 and line an 8x8-inch (20cm) square dish with parchment paper.

2. Add the oats and baking powder to a large bowl and mix with a spoon.

3. Add in the milk, egg, mashed banana or apple sauce, honey and vanilla and mix again.

4. Finally, fold in the frozen berries.

5. Transfer the mixture to the baking dish and cook in the oven for 40 minutes.

6. Allow to cool completely in the dish before removing and cutting into 9 bars.

SMOOTHIE BAGS

| Serves: 2 | Prep time: 2 minutes | Cook time: 2 minutes | Equipment: Blender or smoothie maker |

These make-ahead smoothie packs are super handy to have in the freezer. All the ingredients are pre-measured and bagged up, ready to pop straight into the blender in the morning.

INGREDIENTS

Berry Blitz

200g frozen berries

50g oats

30g fresh baby spinach

Chocolate Chia

1 banana, sliced

100g plain yoghurt

1 tbsp cocoa

½ tbsp chia seeds

Tropical Burst

200g frozen tropical fruit

30g cashew nuts

1 satsuma, peeled

Creamy Banana

2 bananas, sliced

50g diced cauliflower (see page 161)

1 tsp vanilla extract

METHOD

1. Add the ingredients to a freezer bag, push out the air and seal shut.

2. Freeze for up to 2 months.

3. When ready to make, add the contents of the bag, straight from the freezer, to a blender.

4. Add 500–600ml milk of your choice (dairy or non-dairy) and blitz until smooth.

5. Serve immediately.

LUNCH

Sausage Meatball Muffins
Pasta Salad Four Ways
Cheat's Calzone
Mini Pizza Bites
Sausage & Veg Bites
Halloumi & Sweetcorn Fritters
Chicken & Broccoli Fritters
Ham & Cheese Pastry Parcels
Freezer Sandwich Pouches
Chicken Noodle Soup
Curried Squash Soup
Roasted Tomato Soup

SAUSAGE MEATBALL MUFFINS

| Makes: 12 | Prep time: 12 minutes | Cook time: 25 minutes | Equipment: Muffin tin, large jug and large mixing bowl |

These tasty savoury muffins topped with a sausage meatball are ideal to batch-cook and keep in the freezer for lunches all week long.

INGREDIENTS

75g butter

2 medium eggs

150ml milk

150g grated Cheddar cheese

250g self-raising flour

½ tsp dried oregano

½ tsp garlic granules

4 sausages (meat or veggie)

STORING

These muffins can be kept in the fridge for up to 3 days and can either be eaten cold or reheated in the oven or microwave.

FREEZING

To freeze, remove the muffins from their cases and flash freeze on a tray or plate for 1 hour until hard. Transfer to a freezer bag or container and freeze for up to 3 months.

Defrost at room temperature for 4 hours.

METHOD

1. Preheat the oven to 200°C/180°C Fan/ Gas Mark 6 and line a 12-hole muffin tray with parchment paper or silicone cases.

2. Melt the butter in a jug in the microwave and then add in the eggs, milk and cheese, stirring well.

3. Pour this into a large bowl and then add the flour, oregano and garlic granules.

4. Divide the mixture between the 12 muffin cases. I find it easier to do this with an ice cream scoop!

5. Remove the sausages from their skin and make 3 small meatballs from each sausage, giving you 12 in total.

6. Push one sausage meatball down into the muffin mixture so that half is submerged and half is still showing on top. Repeat with all the sausages and muffins.

7. Bake in the oven for 25 minutes until golden brown on top.

PASTA SALAD FOUR WAYS

| Serves: 16 | Prep time: 5 minutes | Cook time: 10 minutes | Equipment: Large saucepan and large mixing bowl |

Pasta salad is a great alternative to sandwiches and is ideal for a packed lunch or to take out and about for a picnic – find a photograph of my options on page 40.

INGREDIENTS

Pizza Pasta Salad

250g pasta

100g cherry tomatoes, chopped

50g cheese, cut into cubes

50g pepperoni

50g black olives, sliced

1 spring onion, chopped

½ tbsp oil

½ tbsp white wine vinegar

1 tsp dried oregano

Mexican Pasta Salad

250g pasta

250g tin mixed beans

1 red pepper, chopped

1 spring onion, chopped

75g cheese, cut into cubes

½ tbsp oil

½ tbsp white wine vinegar

1 tsp dried oregano

½ tsp cumin

Pesto Chickpea Pasta Salad

250g pasta

150g tinned chickpeas, drained

4 tbsp pesto

120g cherry tomatoes, chopped

100g cucumber, cut into cubes

1 ball mozzarella, torn into small pieces

Coronation Chicken Pasta Salad

250g pasta

200g cooked chicken, shredded

100g plain yoghurt

2 tsp mild curry powder

30g fresh baby spinach, chopped

25g raisins

METHOD

1. Add the pasta to a pan of boiling water and cook according to the packet instructions.

2. In the meantime, put the rest of the ingredients into a large bowl and mix.

3. Drain pasta, allow to cool. You can run it under cold water to cool quicker.

4. Mix all the ingredients together until well combined.

STORING

Store the pasta salad in a container or lunch box in the fridge for up to 2 days. Eat cold.

CHEAT'S CALZONE

| Makes: 1 | Prep time: 4 minutes | Cook time: 10 minutes | Equipment: Large baking tray |

Make your own mini calzone pizza at home in less than 15 minutes. I've added cheese, pepperoni and tomatoes to mine, but feel free to use whatever fillings you prefer.

INGREDIENTS

1 mini tortilla wrap

1 tbsp passata or pizza sauce

pinch of dried oregano

25g grated Cheddar cheese

2 slices pepperoni

2 cherry tomatoes, sliced

1 tsp butter

METHOD

1. Preheat the oven to 220°C/200°C Fan/ Gas Mark 7 and line a large baking tray with parchment paper.

2. Lay the tortilla out flat on the tray and on one half spread the passata or pizza sauce. Then sprinkle on the oregano.

3. Add the grated cheese, pepperoni and tomatoes and fold the other half of the wrap over the filling.

4. Use a fork to crimp the edges, pressing them together to seal the wrap shut.

5. Melt the butter and brush it on top. This will also help with crimping the edges.

6. Bake in the oven for 10 minutes.

7. Allow to cool for a few minutes before serving.

STORING

These calzones can be served hot or allowed to cool, put into a lunch box and kept for lunch time. They are best eaten the day they are made but can be kept in the fridge for up to 2 days.

FREEZING

Freeze before cooking. Place the calzone on a plate after Step 5 and flash freeze for 1 hour until hard. Wrap in plastic wrap or foil and transfer to a freezer bag or container and freeze for up to 2 months.

Bake from frozen at 220°C/200°C Fan/Gas Mark 7 for 13 minutes.

MINI PIZZA BITES

| Makes: 12 | Prep time: 5 minutes | Cook time: 8 minutes | Equipment: Muffin tin and pastry cutter or jar |

These Mini Pizza Bites are my daughter's new favourite lunch recipe. We add mozzarella and a chopped-up pepperoni stick which makes mini slices of pepperoni. But feel free to add any toppings you like.

INGREDIENTS

butter or oil, for greasing

3 large tortilla wraps

100g pizza sauce

60g grated mozzarella

6 cherry tomatoes, halved

1 pepperoni stick, chopped

STORING

These pizza bites can be kept in the fridge for up to 2 days and can either be eaten cold or reheated in the oven or microwave.

FREEZING

Defrost at room temperature in 1.5 hours or in the microwave for 45 seconds.

METHOD

1. Preheat the oven to 200°C/180°C Fan/ Gas Mark 6 and grease a 12-hole muffin tin with butter or oil.

2. Use a pastry cutter or jar of about 7 or 8cm in diameter to cut out circles from the tortilla.

3. Press the tortilla circles down into the muffin tray holes.

4. Add a little pizza sauce and some grated mozzarella and top with half a cherry tomato and a few pieces of sliced pepperoni stick.

5. Bake in the oven for 8 minutes and allow to cool for a few minutes before removing from the tray.

SAUSAGE & VEG BITES

DF EF

| Makes: 20 | Prep time: 10 minutes | Cook time: 15 minutes | Equipment: Large baking tray and large mixing bowl |

These little sausage bites are so tasty and are ideal to pop into lunch boxes for a delicious savoury treat.

INGREDIENTS

350g sausages

1 small courgette

1 medium carrot

50g dried breadcrumbs

STORING

These bites will keep in an airtight container in the fridge for 2 days. You can eat these bites cold or reheat in the microwave.

FREEZING

Flash freeze on a tray or plate for 1 hour until hard. Transfer to a freezer bag or container and freeze for up to 2 months.

Defrost in the fridge overnight.

METHOD

1. Preheat the oven to 200°C/180°C Fan/ Gas Mark 6 and line a large baking tray with parchment paper.

2. Take the skins off the sausages and add them to a large bowl.

3. Grate the courgette, squeeze out the water from it and add to the bowl.

4. Then grate the carrot and add that too, along with the breadcrumbs.

5. Mix with a spoon until all the ingredients are combined.

6. Take a heaped tablespoon of the sausage mixture and shape with your hands into a meatball shape.

7. Place on the tray and repeat with the rest of the mixture. You should be able to make about 20.

8. Bake in the oven for 15 minutes and allow to cool for a couple of minutes before serving.

HALLOUMI & SWEETCORN FRITTERS

| Makes: 8 | Prep time: 7 minutes | Cook time: 18 minutes | Equipment: Large mixing bowl and frying pan |

Delicious fritters packed with halloumi and sweetcorn. These are a fantastic way to get kids to try a cheese other than Cheddar!

INGREDIENTS

100g plain flour

1 tsp baking powder

1 medium egg

100ml milk

250g fresh or frozen sweetcorn

100g halloumi, diced

1 spring onion, chopped

1 tbsp oil

STORING

These fritters can be kept in the fridge for up to 3 days and can either be eaten cold or reheated in the oven or microwave.

FREEZING

To freeze, wrap the fritters individually or in twos in plastic wrap or foil. Place all the wrapped fritters into a freezer bag or container and freeze for up to 3 months.

The fritters will defrost at room temperature in 3 hours. Reheat in the microwave.

METHOD

1. Put the flour and baking powder in a large bowl and mix with a spoon.

2. Add the egg and milk and mix well.

3. Add the sweetcorn, halloumi and spring onion and mix until combined.

4. Heat the oil in a non-stick frying pan over a low heat.

5. Add 2 spoonfuls of the fritter mixture to the pan to make 1 fritter. You should be able to cook 4 fritters at a time.

6. Fry on low for 5 minutes, turn and fry on the other side for another 4 minutes.

7. Remove the fritter and leave to rest on some kitchen paper to drain off any excess oil.

8. Fry the remaining fritters and then serve immediately.

CHICKEN & BROCCOLI FRITTERS

| Makes: 8 | Prep time: 8 minutes | Cook time: 23 minutes | Equipment: Large mixing bowl and frying pan |

These delicious cheesy fritters are the only way I can get my kids to eat broccoli!

INGREDIENTS

200g broccoli

300g chicken breasts

100g grated Cheddar cheese

1 medium egg

100ml milk

1 tbsp chopped chives

50g plain flour

salt and pepper (optional)

1 tbsp oil

STORING

These fritters can be kept in the fridge for up to 3 days and can either be eaten cold or reheated in the oven or microwave.

FREEZING

To freeze, wrap the fritters individually or in twos in plastic wrap or foil. Place all the wrapped fritters into a freezer bag or container and freeze for up to 3 months.

The fritters will defrost at room temperature in 3 hours. Reheat in the microwave.

METHOD

1. Chop the broccoli into small florets and steam until soft. If you don't have a steamer, boiling is fine.

2. Whilst the broccoli is cooking, chop the chicken into small, bite-sized pieces and add to a large bowl.

3. Add the cheese, egg, milk and chives to the bowl and mix well.

4. When the broccoli is cooked, remove from the pan and chop into very small pieces.

5. Add the chopped broccoli to the bowl and mix well.

6. Finally, add the flour and mix again. You can season with salt and pepper at this point if you wish.

7. Heat the oil in a non-stick frying pan over a low heat.

8. Add 2 spoonfuls of the fritter mixture to the pan to make 1 fritter. You should be able to cook 4 fritters at a time.

9. Fry on low for 5 minutes, turn and fry on the other side for another 4 minutes.

10. Remove the fritters and leave to rest on some kitchen paper to drain off any excess oil.

11. Fry the remaining fritters and serve immediately.

HAM & CHEESE PASTRY PARCELS

| Makes: 12 | Prep time: 7 minutes | Cook time: 20 minutes | Equipment: Baking trays |

I always pick up a roll of puff pastry at the supermarket. It's so handy to have in the fridge to whip up a tasty lunch treat like these Ham & Cheese Pastry Parcels. Feel free to swap the ham for chicken or turkey slices or vegetarian alternatives.

INGREDIENTS

1 sheet ready-rolled puff pastry

1 tbsp mayonnaise

2 tsp French mustard

12 slices cooked ham

100g grated Cheddar cheese

STORING

These pastry parcels can be kept in the fridge for up to 2 days. They can be reheated in the oven or microwave.

FREEZING

Freeze these parcels before cooking. After completing Step 5, place the uncooked parcels onto a tray or plate ensuring that they are not touching. Freeze for a couple of hours until solid then transfer to a freezer bag or container for up to 2 months.

Bake directly from frozen at 220°C/200°C Fan/Gas Mark 7. Place on a lined baking tray and cook for 25 minutes.

METHOD

1. Preheat the oven to 200°C/180°C Fan/Gas Mark 6 and line 2 baking trays with parchment paper.

2. Unroll the pastry and cut it into 12 squares.

3. Mix the mayonnaise and French mustard in a small bowl and then add a small dollop to each of the pastry squares.

4. Next, put a slice of ham on top and then a small pile of grated cheese.

5. Close the parcel by pulling each corner of the pastry into the middle and pinch a little until the corners meet. Don't worry if they are not even or are a bit messy. They will change shape anyway during cooking!

6. Transfer the parcels onto the lined baking trays. Bake in the oven for 20 minutes and allow to cool for a few minutes before serving.

FREEZER SANDWICH POUCHES

| Makes: 4 | Prep time: 4 minutes | Cook time: 12 minutes | Equipment: Baking tray |

Batch make sandwiches for the whole week. Kids will love these crustless sandwich pouches. And they taste even better baked!

INGREDIENTS

8 slices of bread

1 tbsp butter

4 slices of ham

4 slices of cheese

LUNCH BOX SANDWICHES

These sandwiches will defrost in a couple of hours at room temperature so are ideal to pop into lunch boxes in the morning.

TOASTIES

You can also turn them into toasties by buttering the top and baking them direct from frozen at 200°C/180°C Fan/Gas Mark 6 for 12 minutes.

METHOD

1. Make a ham and cheese sandwich as normal and then use a pastry cutter to cut a circle from the sandwich. You can also use a bowl if you don't have a pastry cutter.

2. Use a fork to push down and seal together the edges of the sandwich. (This step is optional, you can leave the sandwich open if you prefer.)

3. Repeat with the remaining sandwiches and then wrap each one individually in plastic wrap or a bees wax wrap. Put all 4 sandwiches into a freezer bag, push out the air and seal.

4. Freeze for up to 2 months.

CHICKEN NOODLE SOUP

| Serves: 4 | Prep time: 4 minutes | Cook time: 25 minutes | Equipment: Large saucepan |

You can't beat a big bowl of comforting Chicken Noodle Soup on a cold day. I use vermicelli pasta, but if you can't find that at the supermarket then spaghetti will work just as well too.

INGREDIENTS

½ tbsp oil

1 onion, diced

2 garlic cloves, crushed

1 tsp ginger, chopped

3 medium carrots, thinly sliced

2 celery sticks, diced

2 chicken breasts

1 tsp dried oregano

2 litres hot chicken stock

160g sweetcorn (tinned or frozen)

75g vermicelli pasta (or spaghetti)

2 tbsp soy sauce

METHOD

1. Add the oil, onion, garlic, ginger, carrots and celery to a large saucepan on the hob.

2. Sauté for about 3 minutes, stirring regularly.

3. Add chicken breasts, whole, along with the dried oregano and chicken stock.

4. Bring to the boil and then simmer for 20 minutes, until the chicken is cooked through.

5. Remove chicken, shred into small pieces and return to saucepan.

6. Add the sweetcorn, vermicelli (or spaghetti) and soy sauce.

7. Stir and simmer for another 7 minutes or until the pasta is cooked. Serve immediately.

STORING

This soup will keep in an airtight container in the fridge for up to 2 days. Reheat on the hob or in the microwave.

FREEZING

Freeze in bags or containers for up to 3 months. Defrost overnight in the fridge. Reheat on the hob or in the microwave.

CURRIED SQUASH SOUP

| Serves: 4 | Prep Time: 10 minutes | Cook time: 25 minutes | Equipment: Large saucepan and blender |

This butternut squash soup has a delicious creamy texture despite not having any cream in it at all. It's very lightly spiced so perfect for kids and makes a really comforting lunch on a winter's day.

INGREDIENTS

1 small butternut squash or
500g frozen squash chunks

250g potato

1 tbsp oil

1 onion, diced

2 garlic cloves, crushed

1 tbsp mild curry powder

1 litre hot vegetable stock

METHOD

1. If using a fresh butternut squash, peel it and then chop into small bite-sized pieces.

2. Leave the skins on the potato and chop into similar-sized chunks.

3. Add the oil and onion to a large saucepan and sauté for 2–3 minutes.

4. Add the garlic and curry powder and cook for about 30 seconds, stirring constantly.

5. Add the butternut squash, potatoes and vegetable stock, bring to the boil and simmer for about 15–18 minutes until the veggies are soft.

6. Cool slightly, then blitz with a hand blender or transfer to a stand blender. Serve immediately.

STORING

This soup will keep in an airtight container in the fridge for up to 2 days. Reheat on the hob or in the microwave.

FREEZING

Freeze in bags or containers for up to 3 months. Defrost overnight in the fridge. Reheat on the hob or in the microwave.

ROASTED TOMATO SOUP

| Serves: 4 | Prep time: 4 minutes | Cook time: 30 minutes | Equipment: Baking tray, large saucepan and blender |

Roasting tomatoes in the oven with peppers and garlic creates a delicious sweet flavour which makes the most wonderful soup. It can even be used as a pasta sauce for kids who don't like eating soup!

INGREDIENTS

650g vine tomatoes

1 red pepper

3 garlic cloves

1 tbsp oil

½ tsp dried basil

350g potatoes

1 litre vegetable stock

1 tsp smoked paprika

STORING

This soup will keep in an airtight container in the fridge for up to 2 days. Reheat on the hob or in the microwave.

FREEZING

Freeze in bags or containers for up to 3 months. Defrost overnight in the fridge. Reheat on the hob or in the microwave.

METHOD

1. Preheat the oven to 200°C/180°C Fan/ Gas Mark 6.

2. Cut the tomatoes in quarters and add to a baking tray.

3. Cut or tear the red pepper into largish chunks and add that to the tray, along with the garlic cloves, peeled but left whole.

4. Drizzle the olive oil over the top, sprinkle on the dried basil and then mix well.

5. Bake in the oven for 15 minutes.

6. Meanwhile, chop the potatoes into bite-sized chunks, leaving the skins on.

7. When ready, remove the tray from the oven and transfer the contents to a large saucepan.

8. Add the cubed potatoes along with the vegetable stock and smoked paprika.

9. Bring to the boil and cook on a medium simmer for 12–15 minutes until the potatoes are soft.

10. Blitz the soup with a hand or stand blender. Serve immediately.

ONE-POT WONDERS

Lazy Lasagne
Creamy Chicken Curry & Rice
Three Veg Mac & Cheese
Smoky Veggie Chilli
Chicken Alfredo Tagliatelle
Meatball Gnocchi Fake Bake
Chorizo Carbonara
Satay Chicken Noodles
Quick Kung Po

LAZY LASAGNE

| Serves: 4 | Prep time: 10 minutes | Cook time: 25 minutes | Equipment: Large pan or shallow casserole dish |

Take all the stress and hassle out of lasagne by making it all in one pot on the hob.
It's quicker, easier and leaves you with far less washing up!

INGREDIENTS

½ tbsp oil

1 onion

2 garlic cloves, crushed

2 celery sticks, finely diced

1 large carrot, finely diced

500g beef mince (or veggie equivalent)

400g tin chopped tomatoes

450ml beef stock

150ml red wine or more stock

2 tbsp tomato purée

1 tsp dried oregano

200g dried lasagne sheets

100g crème fraîche

25g grated Parmesan

50g grated Cheddar cheese

METHOD

1. Heat the oil in a large pan or casserole dish.

2. Add the onion, garlic, celery and carrots and fry for 2–3 minutes on a medium heat.

3. Add the beef mince and fry for another few minutes until the mince has browned.

4. Add the chopped tomatoes, beef stock, red wine (if using), tomato purée and oregano.

5. Bring the mixture to the boil and then add the lasagne sheets, breaking each into 4 or 5 pieces as you add them in.

6. Simmer on a low heat for about 15 minutes, stirring regularly to ensure that the lasagne sheets don't stick together.

7. Mix the crème fraîche, parmesan and Cheddar together in a bowl and then add to the top of the lasagne in 7 or 8 spoonfuls.

8. Cook for another 2–3 minutes to allow the cheese mixture to heat through and then serve.

STORING

Leftovers can be cooled and kept in a sealed container in the fridge for up to 2 days. Heat thoroughly in the microwave or on the hob before serving.

CREAMY CHICKEN CURRY & RICE

   NF

| Serves: 4 | Prep time: 2 minutes | Cook time: 25 minutes | Equipment: Large pan or shallow casserole dish |

All the delicious flavours of creamy chicken curry and rice but cooked in one pot in less than half an hour.

INGREDIENTS

½ tbsp oil

1 onion diced

2 garlic cloves, crushed

½ tsp chopped ginger

2 tbsp mild curry paste

400g diced chicken breast

800ml chicken stock

400ml tin coconut milk

300g easy-cook long-grain rice

75g fresh baby spinach

STORING

Leftovers can be cooled and kept in a sealed container in the fridge for up to 2 days. Heat thoroughly in the microwave or on the hob before serving.

METHOD

1. Heat the oil in a large pan or casserole dish on a medium heat on the hob.

2. Add the onion, garlic and ginger and sauté for 2–3 minutes until the onions have softened but haven't yet started to brown.

3. Add the curry paste and mix quickly, cooking for about 30 seconds.

4. Add the diced chicken and mix well.

5. Finally add the chicken stock, coconut milk and rice.

6. Bring to the boil, reduce to a simmer and cook for about 15–18 minutes until the rice is fully cooked.

7. Stir every few minutes to prevent the rice from sticking.

8. Remove from the heat and stir in the baby spinach, the heat will wilt it down quickly.

THREE VEG MAC & CHEESE

| Serves: 4 | Prep time: 5 minutes | Cook time: 19 minutes | Equipment: Large pan or shallow casserole dish |

The easiest mac & cheese recipe ever. Everything is cooked in one pot on the hob and finished under the grill. This recipe is also packed with sneaky veg and great for fussy eaters.

INGREDIENTS

400g pasta

550ml vegetable stock

550ml milk

1 tsp dried oregano

1tsp garlic powder

1 medium courgette, grated

150g diced cauliflower – frozen or fresh (see page 161)

1 tsp French mustard

150g grated cheese, plus 25g extra for top

2 tomatoes, sliced

STORING

Leftovers can be cooled and kept in a sealed container in the fridge for up to 2 days. Heat thoroughly in the microwave or on the hob before serving.

METHOD

1. Put the pasta, stock, milk, oregano and garlic powder in a large pan or casserole dish that's suitable to be used on the hob and under the grill.

2. Bring to the boil and simmer for 4-5 minutes.

3. Add the courgette and cauliflower, stir well and cook for another 4-5 minutes until the pasta is fully cooked and most of the liquid has absorbed.

4. Turn off the heat and add the French mustard and grated cheese. Mix well.

5. Sprinkle the remaining grated cheese over the top along with the sliced tomatoes.

6. Put dish under grill for 5 minutes until the cheese has browned and the tomatoes are warm through.

SMOKY VEGGIE CHILLI

| Serves: 4 | Prep time: 2 minutes | Cook time: 20 minutes | Equipment: Large pan or shallow casserole dish |

A tasty and warming one-pot veggie chilli ready in just over 20 minutes.

INGREDIENTS

½ tbsp oil

1 onion, diced

1 garlic clove, crushed

2 tsp chipotle paste

1 tsp ground cumin

1 tsp smoked paprika

400g tin chopped tomatoes

400g tin cooked kidney beans, drained

400g tin cooked black beans, drained

100ml vegetable stock

100g frozen peas and sweetcorn

tortilla chips, sour cream, fresh coriander and grated Cheddar cheese, to serve

METHOD

1. Heat the oil in a large pan or casserole dish.

2. Add the onions and garlic and cook for 2–3 minutes.

3. Add the chipotle paste, ground cumin and smoked paprika, stir well and cook for another minute.

4. Add the chopped tomatoes, kidney beans, black beans and vegetable stock.

5. Bring to the boil and simmer for 8 minutes.

6. Add the frozen peas and sweetcorn and cook for a further 3–4 minutes.

7. Serve immediately with tortilla chips and toppings such as sour cream, fresh coriander and grated Cheddar cheese.

STORING

Leftovers can be cooled and kept in a sealed container in the fridge for up to 2 days. Heat thoroughly in the microwave or on the hob before serving.

CHICKEN ALFREDO TAGLIATELLE

| Serves: 4 | Prep time: 2 minutes | Cook time: 17 minutes | Equipment: Large pan or shallow casserole dish |

A delicious and creamy one-pot chicken pasta dish, ready in less than 20 minutes.

INGREDIENTS

½ tbsp oil

350g chicken breast, diced

1 tsp dried oregano

1 tsp garlic granules

350g tagliatelle

600ml milk

600ml chicken stock

3 tbsp crème fraîche

40g grated Parmesan

chopped parsley, to serve

STORING

Leftovers can be cooled and kept in a sealed container in the fridge for up to 2 days. Heat thoroughly in the microwave or on the hob before serving.

METHOD

1. Put the oil, diced chicken, oregano and garlic in a large pan on the hob.

2. Sauté for 3 minutes over a medium heat to lightly cook the chicken.

3. Add the tagliatelle, milk and chicken stock.

4. Bring to the boil and then simmer for 12 minutes, stirring regularly.

5. By now the pasta should be cooked and the majority of the liquid absorbed.

6. Remove from the heat and stir in the crème fraîche and parmesan.

7. Serve with chopped parsley sprinkled on top.

MEATBALL GNOCCHI FAKE BAKE

| Serves: 4 | Prep time: 2 minutes | Cook time: 25 minutes | Equipment: Shallow casserole dish or large frying pan |

All the great taste and flavour of baked meatballs and gnocchi but made super-quick and easy on the hob and under the grill.

INGREDIENTS

½ tbsp oil

350g beef meatballs

1 red pepper, chopped

2 garlic cloves, crushed

400g tin chopped tomatoes

200ml beef stock

1 tbsp Worcestershire sauce

1 tsp dried oregano

500g gnocchi

100g frozen peas

50g grated Cheddar cheese

50g grated mozzarella

STORING

Leftovers can be cooled and kept in a sealed container in the fridge for up to 2 days. Heat thoroughly in the microwave or on the hob before serving.

METHOD

1. Put the oil and meatballs in a large pan or casserole dish that's suitable to be used on the hob or the grill.

2. Cook for 5 minutes, turning the meatballs regularly to brown on all sides.

3. Add the red pepper and garlic and cook for another minute.

4. Add the chopped tomatoes, beef stock, Worcestershire sauce and oregano.

5. Bring to the boil and simmer for 10 minutes.

6. Add the gnocchi and peas and cook for a further 5 minutes, stirring a few times.

7. Sprinkle the Cheddar and mozzarella on top and place the pan under the grill for 4-5 minutes until nicely browned.

CHORIZO CARBONARA

NF

Far from authentic, my one-pot carbonara merges an Italian favourite with a Spanish twist. A little unusual but super-delicious!

INGREDIENTS

100g chorizo

350g spaghetti

1 litre vegetable stock

2 cloves garlic, crushed

1 large courgette

125ml single cream

2 eggs

50g grated Parmesan

STORING

Leftovers can be cooled and kept in a sealed container in the fridge for up to 2 days. Heat thoroughly in the microwave or on the hob before serving.

METHOD

1. Chop the chorizo into small pieces and add to a large frying pan or shallow casserole dish.

2. Fry for 4–5 minutes on medium heat until crisp.

3. Remove the chorizo, but keep any remaining oils in the pan.

4. Add the spaghetti, vegetable stock and garlic.

5. Bring to the boil and cook for about 5 minutes, stirring regularly so that the spaghetti doesn't stick.

6. Meanwhile, use a vegetable peeler to peel the courgette into thin strips. Add these to the spaghetti and cook for another 3–4 minutes.

7. Put the cream, eggs and Parmesan in a jug and mix well.

8. When the spaghetti is cooked and the stock is nearly all absorbed, remove the pan from the heat and stir in the cream mixture. Mix quickly to avoid over-cooking the egg.

9. Serve immediately with the crispy chorizo croutons on top.

SATAY CHICKEN NOODLES

DF

| Serves: 4 | Prep time: 5 minutes | Cook time: 18 minutes | Equipment: Large frying pan or shallow casserole dish |

Creamy chicken satay and vegetables all cooked together in one pan with noodles.

INGREDIENTS

400g chicken thighs (skinless and boneless)

½ tbsp oil

1 tbsp mild curry paste

75g crunchy peanut butter

400ml tin coconut milk

1 tbsp soy sauce

100g sugar snap peas

150g baby corn

1 red pepper, chopped

300g straight-to-wok noodles

STORING

Leftovers can be cooled and kept in a sealed container in the fridge for up to 2 days. Heat thoroughly in the microwave or on the hob before serving.

METHOD

1. Chop the chicken thighs into bite sized pieces.

2. Add them to a large frying pan or casserole dish on the hob along with the oil and curry paste and cook for 3–4 minutes.

3. Add the peanut butter, coconut milk and soy sauce and mix well.

4. Add the sugar snap peas, baby corn and red pepper and cook for about 5 minutes.

5. Finally add the noodles and cook for 3–4 minutes, stirring constantly to break down the noodles into the sauce, until the veggies are soft and the chicken is cooked through.

QUICK KUNG PO

| Serves: 4 | Prep time: 5 minutes | Cook time: 20 minutes | Equipment: Wok or large frying pan |

This healthier twist on a takeaway recipe is sure to become your new mid-week favourite.
Serve with microwave rice to keep it speedy and easy!

INGREDIENTS

1 tbsp oil

400g diced chicken breast

1 onion, cut into largish chunks

2 garlic cloves, crushed

2 peppers, cut into largish chunks

100g mangetout

200ml chicken stock

2 tbsp soy sauce

2 tbsp sweet chilli sauce

2 tbsp tomato purée

1 tbsp rice wine vinegar

1 tbsp honey

50g cashew nuts

boiled or microwave rice, to serve

METHOD

1. Add the oil and chicken to a wok or large frying
    pan and cook for about 5-6 minutes until the
    chicken has browned.

2. Add the onion, garlic, peppers and mangetout
    and cook for another 2 minutes.

3. Mix the chicken stock, soy sauce, sweet chilli
    sauce, tomato purée, rice wine vinegar and honey
    together in a jug and pour into the wok.

4. Mix well and cook for about 10 minutes until
    the veggies are soft and the chicken is cooked
    through.

5. Remove from the heat and stir in the cashew nuts.

6. Serve with rice.

STORING

Leftovers can be cooled and kept
in a sealed container in the fridge
for up to 2 days. Heat thoroughly in
the microwave or on the hob before
serving, and pair with a packet of
microwave rice.

FAMILY FAVOURITES

Parmesan Chicken Goujons
Mixed Fish Bites
Veggie Nuggets
Two-Ingredient Pizza Dough
Fish & Chip Pie
Sausage & Veg Traybake
Turkey Chilli Burrito Bowl
Cheddar & Veg Pot Pies
Chinese Chicken Curry
Swedish Meatballs
Crispy Chicken Burgers
Spinach & Cottage Cheese Cannelloni
Greek Chicken Kebab
Sausage Jambalaya
Sticky Chicken & Rainbow Rice

PARMESAN CHICKEN GOUJONS

| Serves: 4 | Prep time: 10 minutes | Cook time: 17 minutes | Equipment: Baking tray |

What's not to love about a chicken nugget? My recipe uses chicken mini fillets to create these tasty Parmesan-crusted goujons. Super kid-friendly and great to have in the freezer for busy days.

INGREDIENTS

2 eggs

50g dried breadcrumbs

25g grated Parmesan

450g chicken mini fillets

1 tbsp oil

STORING

These goujons are best eaten immediately after cooking but they will keep in the fridge for up to 2 days and can be reheated in the oven or microwave.

FREEZING

Freeze the goujons before cooking. After Step 5, place the goujons on a tray or plate and flash freeze for 1 hour until hard. Transfer to a freezer bag or container and freeze for up to 2 months.

Cook directly from frozen. Brush a little oil on top of the goujons and cook in the oven for at least 20 minutes or in an air fryer for at least 17 minutes.

METHOD

1. Preheat the oven to 220°C/200°C Fan/ Gas Mark 7 and line a baking tray with parchment paper.

2. Crack the eggs into bowl and whisk with a fork.

3. Add the breadcrumbs and Parmesan to another bowl and mix.

4. Take one of the chicken mini fillets, dip it in the egg and then coat in the breadcrumb mixture.

5. Place the coated chicken on the tray and repeat with the remaining mini fillets.

6. Brush a little of the oil on top of the goujons and bake in the oven for 17 minutes.

7. You can also cook them in the air fryer for approximately 15 minutes depending on the model of air fryer you are using.

MIXED FISH BITES

| Serves: 4 | Prep time: 10 minutes | Cook time: 15 minutes | Equipment: Baking tray |

It's not always easy to get children to eat fish but coating them in crispy panko breadcrumbs is a great way to introduce them to different types and flavours of fish. I use a packet of fish pie mix for ease. The fish has already been skinned and chopped, but feel free to do this yourself if you prefer.

INGREDIENTS

50g plain flour

2 eggs

50g panko breadcrumbs

1 tsp dried oregano

450g fish pie mix (salmon, cod and haddock)

1 tbsp oil

STORING

These fish bites are best eaten immediately after cooking but they will keep in the fridge for up to 2 days and can be reheated in the oven or microwave.

FREEZING

Freeze the fish bites before cooking. After Step 6, place the bites on a tray or plate and flash freeze for 1 hour until hard. Transfer to a freezer bag or container and freeze for up to 2 months.

Cook directly from frozen. Brush a little oil on top of the fish bites and cook in the oven for at least 18 minutes or in an air fryer for at least 15 minutes.

METHOD

1. Preheat the oven to 220°C/200°C Fan/ Gas Mark 7 and line a baking tray with parchment paper.

2. Add the flour to one bowl.

3. Crack the eggs into a second bowl and whisk with a fork.

4. Add the panko breadcrumbs and dried oregano to a third bowl and mix.

5. Take one piece of fish, coat it in the flour, dip it in the egg and then sprinkle on the breadcrumbs.

6. Place the coated fish on the tray and repeat with the remaining pieces of fish.

7. Brush the top of the fish bites with a little oil and bake in the oven for 15 minutes.

8. You can also cook them in the air fryer for approximately 12 minutes depending on the model of air fryer you are using.

VEGGIE NUGGETS

| Serves: 4 | Prep time: 15 minutes | Cook time: 25 minutes | Equipment: Food processor and lined baking tray |

These nuggets are brilliant for veggie-hating kids. Inside their crispy coating they're hiding three different vegetables. Ideal for picky eaters!

INGREDIENTS

120g breadcrumbs

150g broccoli

150g cauliflower

3 medium carrots

150g grated Cheddar cheese

1 egg

1 tsp dried oregano

1 tsp garlic granules

1 tbsp oil

STORING

These nuggets are best eaten immediately after cooking but they will keep in the fridge for up to 2 days and can be reheated in the oven or microwave.

FREEZING

It's best to freeze these nuggets after cooking. Place the cooked nuggets on tray or plate and flash freeze for 1 hour until hard. Transfer to a freezer bag or container and freeze for up to 2 days.

Defrost in the fridge for 4 hours and reheat in the microwave or by frying gently.

METHOD

1. Take half the breadcrumbs and spread them out onto a large plate.

2. Put the broccoli, cauliflower and carrots in a food processor and blitz until the veggies have been broken down to a finer consistency.

3. Add the grated cheese, the remainder of the breadcrumbs, egg, oregano and garlic and blitz again.

4. Take 2 tablespoons of the mixture and shape with your hands into a roundish nugget shape. Dip in the breadcrumbs and then place on a baking tray or plate.

5. Repeat with the remainder of the mixture. You should be able to make 20-25 nuggets depending on their size.

6. You can bake the nuggets in the oven on the lined baking tray. Brush them with a little oil and bake at 220°C/200°C Fan/Gas Mark 7 for 25 minutes.

7. Personally, I think they are much nicer fried. Heat the oil in a frying pan and fry them in batches for about 10 minutes, turning once.

TWO-INGREDIENT PIZZA DOUGH

| Serves: 4 | Prep time: 15 minutes | Cook time: 10 minutes | Equipment: Baking tray or pizza tray and large mixing bowl |

This is possibly the easiest pizza dough recipe ever. Just two simple ingredients and no proving needed!

INGREDIENTS

350g self-raising flour

300g plain Greek yoghurt

STORING

This pizza dough will keep wrapped in plastic wrap in the fridge for 24 hours although it's best to use it as soon as possible.

FREEZING

Freeze the uncooked pizza dough in individual portions for up to 2 months, wrapped in plastic wrap and then placed in a freezer bag or container. Defrost at room temperature in about 3 hours.

METHOD

1. Preheat the oven to 220°C/200°C Fan/ Gas Mark 7. Cut out a sheet of parchment paper the same size as your baking tray or pizza tray.

2. Add the flour and yoghurt to a large bowl and mix well.

3. Once it starts to form into a ball, remove from the bowl and put onto a floured surface.

4. Knead the dough for about a minute and then cut into 4 equal-sized pieces.

5. Take one of those pieces of dough and put it onto the parchment paper.

6. Roll or stretch the dough out into the shape that you want it. The thinner the better!

7. Add whatever toppings you like and then lift the paper onto the baking or pizza tray.

8. Bake for 10–12 minutes and repeat the above steps with the remaining pizza dough.

FISH & CHIP PIE

| Serves: 4 | Prep time: 2 minutes | Cook time: 50 minutes | Equipment: Saucepan and baking dish |

Fish pie, but with a twist! Instead of spending ages peeling, cooking and mashing potatoes for the top, try using frozen chips instead. So easy and the kids will love it!

INGREDIENTS

50g butter

50g flour

500ml milk

75g grated Cheddar cheese

1 tsp French mustard

½ tsp garlic granules

340g fish pie mix (salmon, cod and smoked haddock)

100g frozen prawns

100g cherry tomatoes

100g frozen peas

500g frozen chips (thick-cut)

STORING

This fish pie will keep in the fridge for up to 2 days and can be reheated in the microwave.

FREEZING

Prep all of the steps then freeze the pie in its dish. Cook from frozen at 200°C/180°C Fan/Gas Mark 6 for 75-90 minutes. After about 45 minutes cover the top of the dish loosely with foil to prevent the chips from over-browning.

METHOD

1. Preheat the oven to 200°C/180°C Fan/ Gas Mark 6.

2. Add the butter to a saucepan and melt on the hob over a medium heat.

3. Add in the flour and cook for 1 minute, stirring the whole time.

4. Slowly pour in the milk and whisk well, ensuring there are no lumps of flour left.

5. Cook the sauce for a minute or two until it starts to thicken.

6. Add the grated cheese, French mustard and garlic granules and mix well. The sauce should be thicker now. Remove the pan from the heat.

7. In an oven dish add the fish pie mix, frozen prawns, cherry tomatoes and frozen peas.

8. Pour the sauce over the top and mix everything together.

9. Finally, layer chips on top and bake in the oven for 40 minutes.

SAUSAGE & VEG TRAYBAKE

| Serves: 4 | Prep time: 5 minutes | Cook time: 50 minutes | Equipment: Large, deep baking tray or dish and large jug |

I love meals that you can chuck in the oven and forget about until it's ready. This Sausage & Veg Traybake is one of those. So simple but super tasty. A new family favourite!

INGREDIENTS

600g baby new potatoes

1 onion, roughly chopped

2 garlic cloves, crushed

2 large carrots, thinly sliced

150g cherry tomatoes

1 tsp dried oregano

1 tsp smoked paprika

25g butter

25g flour

350ml hot stock (chicken, beef or veg)

8 sausages

100g fresh baby spinach

STORING

This traybake will keep in the oven for up to 2 days and can be reheated in the microwave.

FREEZING

Cook a double batch, leave it to cool then pop into a freezer bag or container. Freeze flat for up to 3 months.

Defrost in the fridge overnight and reheat in individual portions in the microwave or put it all back in the baking tray and reheat in the oven.

METHOD

1. Preheat the oven to 200°C/180°C Fan/ Gas Mark 6.

2. Leaving the skins on, chop the potatoes in half and add to a large, deep baking tray.

3. Add the onion, garlic, carrots, cherry tomatoes, dried oregano and paprika and mix well.

4. Put the butter in a jug and melt in the microwave.

5. Add the flour to the jug and mix well until it forms a paste.

6. Slowly add the stock to the jug, stirring continuously to remove any lumps.

7. Pour this into the tray and mix everything together.

8. Place the sausages on top and then cook in the oven for 45–50 minutes, turning the sausages once.

9. Remove from the oven and stir in the baby spinach, the heat of the food will wilt it down.

TURKEY CHILLI BURRITO BOWL

| Serves: 4 | Prep time: 5 minutes | Cook time: 27 minutes | Equipment: Large frying pan or shallow casserole dish |

Burritos are so delicious, but can be a bit tricky (not to mention messy!) for kids to eat. Instead I serve mine using the tortilla as an edible bowl for the chilli. But you can, of course, fill the wraps up and eat them as normal if you wish.

INGREDIENTS

½ tbsp oil

1 onion, finely diced

2 garlic cloves, crushed

500g turkey mince

1 tsp smoked paprika

1 tsp ground coriander

1 tsp ground cumin

½ tsp mild chilli powder

2 medium carrots, grated

1 small courgette, grated

400g tin chopped tomatoes

400g tin cooked kidney beans, drained

200ml vegetable stock

2 tbsp tomato purée

25g dark chocolate

250g pouch microwave rice

4 mini tortilla wraps

grated cheese, avocado, red pepper and fresh coriander, to serve

METHOD

1. Heat the oil in a large frying pan or shallow casserole dish on the hob.

2. Add the onion, garlic and turkey mince and cook for 3-4 minutes on medium heat.

3. Add the smoked paprika, ground coriander, ground cumin and chilli powder and mix well. Cook for another minute.

4. Add the grated carrot and courgette, chopped tomatoes, kidney beans, vegetable stock and tomato purée and mix well.

5. Finally, stir in the chocolate until it has melted and then cook on a low simmer for 15 minutes.

6. Add the rice directly into the pan (no need to microwave first) and cook for a further 5 minutes.

7. Push each of the mini tortilla wraps into their own bowls and top with the turkey chilli.

8. Serve with all your favourite toppings.

STORING

Leftovers can be kept in the fridge for up to 2 days and reheated in the microwave.

FREEZING

Freeze the chilli (without the wraps) in containers or freezer bags for up to 3 months. Defrost in the fridge overnight and then reheat in the microwave or on the hob.

CHEDDAR & VEG POT PIES

Serves: 4 | Prep time: 5 minutes | Cook time: 45 minutes | Equipment: Large saucepan or large frying pan, small pie pots or ramekins or large pie dish |

These delicious cheesy vegetable pies are fantastic to have in the freezer ready
to chuck into the oven for meat-free meal days.

INGREDIENTS

½ tbsp oil

1 onion, finely diced

2 garlic cloves, crushed

2 medium carrots, finely diced

3 tsp flour

400ml milk

200ml vegetable stock

200g broccoli, broken into florets

50g frozen peas

50g sweetcorn (fresh or frozen)

100g grated Cheddar cheese

1 sheet ready-rolled puffed pastry

1 egg or 50ml milk (dairy or non-dairy)

STORING

Leftovers can be kept in the fridge
for up to 2 days and reheated in the
microwave.

FREEZING

Pies can be frozen after assembling
but before baking. After Step 10, wrap
the top in plastic wrap then a
layer of foil and freeze flat for up to
3 months. To cook, brush the top with
beaten egg/milk. Bake direct from
frozen at the temps above – 35 mins
for small and up to 50 mins for large.

METHOD

1. Preheat the oven to 200°C/180°C Fan/
   Gas Mark 6.

2. Add the oil, onion, garlic and carrot to a large
   saucepan or large frying pan on the hob and cook
   for 3-4 minutes on medium heat.

3. Add the flour, quickly stirring and cook for about
   30 seconds.

4. Slowly add the milk then the vegetable stock,
   whisking continuously.

5. Bring to the boil and reduce to a simmer.

6. Add in the broccoli, peas and sweetcorn and
   cook for 10-12 minutes until the vegetables are
   soft.

7. Remove from the heat and stir in the grated
   cheese.

8. Divide the mixture between 4 small pie pots or
   ramekins or 1 large pie dish.

9. Cut the puff pastry to a size just slightly larger
   than the dish, pushing the edges of the pastry
   down the sides.

10. Pierce the top with a fork a few times.

11. Brush the top with a little beaten egg or milk.

12. Bake in the oven for 25 minutes for smaller pies
    and up to 35 minutes for one large pie.

CHINESE CHICKEN CURRY

| Serves: 4 | Prep time: 5 minutes | Cook time: 35 minutes | Equipment: Large saucepan and blender |

This recipe is my homemade version of the delicious rich Chicken Curry that you can get at a takeaway. The secret to the flavour is the apples. Trust me, it works!

INGREDIENTS

½ tbsp oil

1 onion, diced

2 small apples, peeled and chopped

1 clove of garlic, chopped

1 tbsp plain flour

1 tbsp mild curry powder

500ml chicken stock

1 tbsp soy sauce

400g chicken breast, diced

2 large carrots, thinly sliced

120g frozen peas

boiled rice, to serve

STORING

This curry will keep in a sealed container in the fridge for up to 2 days. Reheat thoroughly in the microwave or on the hob.

FREEZING

This curry is ideal to freeze in bags or containers for up to 3 months. You can also just make the sauce (up to Step 5) and freeze that. Defrost overnight in the fridge and reheat until piping hot.

METHOD

1. Sauté the oil and onions in a large saucepan for 2–3 minutes or until the onions have softened.

2. Add the apples and garlic and continue to cook for another minute.

3. Add the flour and curry powder and quickly mix, cooking for about 30 seconds.

4. Add the chicken stock and soy sauce, bring to the boil and simmer for 10 minutes.

5. At this point you need to blitz the sauce to make it smooth. You can either use a hand blender or transfer the sauce into a stand blender to blitz.

6. Once the sauce is smooth, add the chicken breast and carrots and simmer for 15–18 minutes until both are cooked through.

7. Add the frozen peas and cook for another 2 minutes.

8. Serve with boiled rice.

SWEDISH MEATBALLS

| Serves: 4 | Prep time: 15 minutes | Cook time: 25 minutes | Equipment: Large mixing bowl and large frying pan |

These Swedish-inspired pork meatballs, cooked in a creamy sauce, are the ultimate comfort food. Serve with mashed potato or even pasta.

INGREDIENTS

500g pork mince

30g dried breadcrumbs

1 egg

1 tsp garlic powder

1 tsp onion powder

2 tbsp oil

2 tbsp butter

2 tbsp plain flour

400ml hot beef stock

100ml single cream

mashed potato or pasta, to serve

STORING

Leftovers can be cooled and kept in a sealed container in the fridge for up to 2 days. Heat thoroughly in the microwave or on the hob before serving.

FREEZING

Freeze in containers or freezer bags for up to 3 months. Defrost in the fridge overnight and then reheat in the microwave or on the hob.

METHOD

1. Add the pork mince, breadcrumbs, egg, garlic powder and onion powder to a large bowl and mix well.

2. Roll the mixture into 20 equal-sized meatballs.

3. Heat the oil in a large frying pan or shallow saucepan. Add 10 of the meatballs and fry for about 6 minutes, turning to ensure all sides are browned.

4. Transfer the meatballs to a bowl and repeat with the remaining 10.

5. Once all meatballs are browned and in a separate bowl, wipe the pan with some kitchen paper to remove any remaining oil.

6. Add the butter to the pan and melt, then add the flour. Mix quickly and cook for a minute before slowly adding beef stock.

7. Whisk until the sauce is smooth and without any lumps.

8. When the sauce starts to thicken, add the meatballs back to the pan and cook for 5 minutes.

9. Remove from the heat and stir in the cream.

10. Serve with mashed potato or pasta.

CRISPY CHICKEN BURGERS

| Serves: 4 | Prep time: 15 minutes | Cook time: 30 minutes | Equipment: Baking tray |

These chicken burgers are my ultimate Friday-night feast meal. The cornflakes give an incredible crispy coating to the chicken and they are perfect to make in bulk and keep in the freezer for another day.

INGREDIENTS

2 large chicken breasts

40g plain flour

2 eggs

100g cornflakes

1 tsp garlic granules

1 tsp onion powder

1 tsp smoked paprika

1 tsp ground cumin

2 tbsp oil

burger bun, mayonnaise, lettuce, tomato and onion, to serve

STORING

These burgers are best eaten immediately after cooking.

FREEZING

Freeze burgers before cooking. After Step 8, place on a tray or plate and flash freeze for 1 hour. Wrap each individually in foil and transfer to a freezer bag or container for up to 2 months. Cook directly from frozen. Place the burgers on a lined baking tray and bake at temps above for about 40 mins. Ensure they are completely cooked through before serving.

METHOD

1. Preheat the oven to 220°C/200°C Fan/ Gas Mark 7 and line a baking tray with parchment paper.

2. Put the chicken breasts between two sheets of parchment paper or plastic wrap and bash with a rolling pin to flatten.

3. Try to get the chicken as even as possible in thickness, then cut each breast in two, giving you four pieces of chicken in total.

4. Add the flour to a bowl.

5. Crack the eggs into a second bowl and whisk.

6. Add the cornflakes to a third bowl and crush with your hands to break them down a little. Then mix in the garlic granules, onion powder, smoked paprika and ground cumin. Stir in the oil and get the cornflakes as evenly coated as possible.

7. Take one piece of chicken, coat it in the flour, dip in the egg and then sprinkle on the cornflake mixture.

8. Place on the baking tray and repeat with the other 3 pieces of chicken.

9. Bake in the oven for 30 minutes until cooked through.

10. Serve in a burger bun with lettuce, tomato, onion and mayo, or whatever your preferences are.

SPINACH & COTTAGE CHEESE CANNELLONI

| Serves: 4 | Prep time: 15 minutes | Cook time: 35 minutes | Equipment: Large baking dish and large jug |

Instead of using ricotta like in the classic recipe, I've used cottage cheese to make the delicious creamy spinach filling for these cannelloni pasta tubes. It takes a little time and effort to make this dish but the final result is well worth it!

INGREDIENTS

1 tbsp butter, plus extra for greasing

300g frozen spinach

300g cottage cheese

25g grated Parmesan

small pinch black pepper

16 dried cannelloni tubes

2 tins chopped tomatoes

150ml hot vegetable stock

1 tbsp balsamic vinegar

1 tsp dried oregano

75g grated Cheddar cheese

STORING

Leftovers can be kept in the fridge for up to 2 days and reheated in the microwave.

FREEZING

An ideal recipe to double up, freezing one batch. Complete all steps above but instead of baking allow to cool, cover in plastic wrap then foil and freeze flat for up to 2 months.

Cook directly from frozen at the temps above for 75-90 mins. After 45 mins cover the top of the dish loosely with foil to prevent cheese burning.

METHOD

1. Preheat the oven to 200°C/180°C Fan/ Gas Mark 6 and lightly grease a large baking dish.

2. Put the frozen spinach in a large jug or bowl and cover with boiling water. Cook in the microwave for about 5 minutes until defrosted. Drain well and squeeze the spinach to remove all excess water.

3. Put the spinach in a bowl along with the cottage cheese, Parmesan and black pepper and mix well.

4. Stuff the cannelloni tubes with the spinach mixture. I find this easiest to do with a small teaspoon and using a chopstick to push it all the way in.

5. Place the stuffed tubes in the baking dish.

6. In another large bowl or jug add the tins of chopped tomatoes, vegetable stock, butter, balsamic vinegar and oregano and mix well.

7. Pour this mixture over the stuffed cannelloni tubes and then top with the grated cheese.

8. Bake in the oven for 30 minutes, covering the top of the dish loosely with foil if the cheese starts to burn.

GREEK CHICKEN KEBAB

Serves: 8 | Prep time: 4 hours | Cook time: 90 minutes | Equipment: Large non-metal mixing bowl, large baking tray and two long metal food skewers |

My homemade chicken kebab recipe is a brilliant show-stopper to serve up to a crowd. If you're cooking it just for your own family there will be loads of leftovers ready to freeze for a meal another day.

INGREDIENTS

Chicken kebab:

500g plain Greek yoghurt

1 tbsp olive oil

2 tsp dried oregano

2 tsp smoked paprika

2 tsp garlic granules

juice of 1 lemon

salt and pepper

1.2kg chicken thighs (skinless and boneless)

Tzatziki:

150g plain Greek yoghurt

¼ cucumber, finely diced

1 garlic clove, crushed

salt and pepper

toasted pitta bread, lettuce, tomato, cucumber, to serve

STORING

Leftovers can be kept in the fridge for up to 2 days and reheated in the microwave.

FREEZING

Put the kebab slices into a freezer container or bag and freeze for up to 3 months. Defrost in the fridge overnight and reheat in microwave.

METHOD

1. Put the Greek yoghurt, olive oil, oregano, paprika, garlic and lemon juice in a large non-metal bowl and mix well. Season with a little salt and pepper.

2. Add the chicken thighs and mix so that they are fully coated in the marinade.

3. Cover the bowl and refrigerate for at least 4 hours or overnight.

4. When ready to cook, preheat the oven to 200°C/180°C Fan/Gas Mark 6 and double line a baking tray with tin foil.

5. Take one of the metal skewers and start to skewer the chicken thighs onto it. Aim to skewer just slightly left of the centre of the thigh.

6. When all the chicken thighs have been skewered, place them onto the lined large baking tray.

7. Take the second skewer and push that through the thighs just slightly right of the centre.

8. This will secure the meat really well.

9. Bake in the oven for 90 minutes. Check the centre of the kebab to ensure it is fully cooked all the way through.

10. Transfer the whole kebab onto a large chopping board and cut slices of the meat from it.

11. To make the tzatziki, in a small bowl mix the yoghurt, cucumber and garlic. Season to taste with salt and pepper.

12. Serve with toasted pitta breads, lettuce, tomato and cucumber.

SAUSAGE JAMBALAYA

| Serves: 4 | Prep time: 3 minutes | Cook time: 35 minutes | Equipment: Large frying pan or shallow casserole dish |

This one-pan sausage and rice dish is my go-to on busy evenings. Easy to make, all in one pan and always a hit with the kids! You can use pork, chicken or veggie sausages.

INGREDIENTS

½ tbsp oil

8 sausages

1 onion, diced

1 garlic clove, crushed

2 peppers, sliced

300g easy-cook long-grain rice

400g tin chopped tomatoes

800ml stock (chicken or vegetable)

1 tsp smoked paprika

100g frozen peas

STORING

Leftovers can be kept in the fridge for up to 2 days and reheated on the hob or in the microwave.

FREEZING

Freeze in containers or freezer bags for up to 3 months. Defrost in the fridge overnight and then reheat in the microwave or on the hob.

METHOD

1. Put oil in a large frying pan or shallow casserole dish.

2. Cut each of the sausages into three (or smaller if you have young children) and add to the pan.

3. Cook for about 4 minutes until they are browned, turning regularly.

4. Add the onion, garlic and peppers and cook for another minute.

5. Add the rice, chopped tomatoes, stock and paprika and mix well.

6. Bring to the boil, reduce to a simmer and cook for 20-25 minutes until the rice is soft.

7. Feel free to add a little extra stock at any point if the jambalaya is looking a little dry, and stir several times to prevent the rice from sticking to the bottom of the pan.

8. Add the frozen peas and cook for a further 4-5 minutes.

9. Serve immediately.

STICKY CHICKEN & RAINBOW RICE

| Serves: 4 | Prep time: 5 minutes | Cook time: 17 minutes | Equipment: Saucepan and large frying pan or wok |

My kids love this sweet and sticky chicken served up with colourful rainbow veggie rice.

INGREDIENTS

For the rice:
300g easy-cook long-grain rice
1 vegetable stock cube
125g mixed frozen vegetables

For the chicken:
400g chicken mini fillets
2 tsp cornflour
1 tsp Chinese five-spice powder
1 tbsp oil
2 tbsp soy sauce
2 tbsp sweet chilli sauce
2 tbsp ketchup
1 tbsp honey
1 tsp sesame seeds

STORING

Leftovers can be kept in the fridge for up to 2 days and reheated in the microwave. Be sure to cool any leftover rice as quickly as you can and put in the fridge as soon as possible.

FREEZING

Both the rice and the chicken can be frozen seperately for up to 3 months. Defrost in the fridge overnight and reheat in the microwave or on the hob.

METHOD

1. Rinse the rice a couple of times under a running tap to remove the starch.

2. Add the rice to a saucepan and cook according to the packet instructions, adding the vegetable stock cube at the beginning.

3. In the last 3-4 minutes of cooking, add the frozen vegetables.

4. Meanwhile, prep the chicken by adding the mini fillets to a bowl along with the cornflour and Chinese five-spice. Mix well so that the chicken is completely coated.

5. Heat the oil in a large frying pan or wok and add the coated chicken. Fry for 8-10 minutes until fully cooked.

6. Remove the chicken from the pan onto a plate and add the soy sauce, sweet chilli sauce, ketchup and honey to the frying pan.

7. Use a whisk to quickly mix the sauce together and cook for 3-4 minutes until the sauce has thickened.

8. Put the chicken back in and cook for another minute, ensuring that it is fully coated in the sauce.

9. Remove from the heat and sprinkle the sesame seeds on top.

10. By now the rice will be cooked and all can be served together.

SLOW COOKER

Chicken Tacos
Mushroom Stroganoff
Beef Ragù
Cauliflower Mac & Cheese
Veggie Bolognese
Beef Casserole
Chicken Casserole
Sausage Casserole
Thai Potato Curry

For a quick note on slow cookers,
see page 15.

CHICKEN TACOS

| Serves: 4 | Prep time: 5 minutes | Cook time: 3-6 hours | Equipment: Slow cooker |

Zesty chicken tacos cooked in the slow cooker and topped with all your favourite toppings. These are sure to be a new mid-week favourite!

INGREDIENTS

1 tsp mild chilli powder

1 tsp ground cumin

½ tsp smoked paprika

500g chicken breasts

400g tin chopped tomatoes

2 garlic cloves, crushed

1 red onion, sliced

3 peppers, sliced

juice of 1 lime

taco shells,

shredded lettuce, shredded cabbage (white or red), fresh coriander,

guacamole, grated Cheddar cheese and wedges of lime, to serve

METHOD

1. Mix the chilli powder, ground cumin and paprika in a small bowl.

2. Place the chicken on a plate and coat in the spice mix, rubbing it in well to the meat.

3. Add the tinned tomatoes, garlic, onion and peppers to the slow cooker and mix.

4. Add the chicken on top and then squeeze over the lime juice.

5. Cook for 3-4 hours on high or 4-6 hours on low.

6. Take 2 forks and shred the chicken into small pieces.

7. Serve immediately with taco shells and all your favourite toppings.

STORING

Leftovers can be kept in the fridge for up to 2 days and reheated in the microwave.

FREEZING

Put the chicken filling in a freezer bag or container and freeze for up to 3 months. Defrost in the fridge overnight and reheat in the microwave or on the hob.

MUSHROOM STROGANOFF

| Serves: 4 | Prep time: 3 minutes | Cook time: 2.5–3.5 hours | Equipment: Slow cooker |

If you are a mushroom lover then this is an absolute must-try recipe.
A deliciously creamy mushroom and pasta stroganoff.

INGREDIENTS

500ml hot vegetable stock

50g butter

1 tsp French mustard

1 onion, diced

2 garlic cloves, crushed

400g mushrooms, roughly chopped

½ tsp dried thyme

salt and pepper

300g pasta

150ml milk

2 tbsp crème fraîche

METHOD

1. Add the vegetable stock, butter and French mustard to the slow cooker and mix well.

2. Add onion, garlic, mushrooms and thyme, along with a little salt and pepper and stir again.

3. Cook on high for 1.5 hours or low for 2.5 hours.

4. Add the pasta and milk, mix well and cook for another hour on high.

5. Turn off the heat and stir in the crème fraîche.

6. Serve immediately.

STORING

Leftovers can be cooled and kept in a sealed container in the fridge for up to 2 days. Heat thoroughly in the microwave or on the hob before serving.

FREEZING

Freeze in containers or freezer bags for up to 2 months. Defrost in the fridge overnight and then reheat in the microwave or on the hob.

BEEF RAGÙ

| Serves: 4 | Prep time: 2 minutes | Cook time: 5-8 hours | Equipment: Slow Cooker |

The key to a rich and flavoursome Italian ragù is a long and slow cook. This recipe contains simple ingredients, but they transform into the most delicious family meal that will have everyone licking their bowl!

INGREDIENTS

1 onion, diced

2 garlic cloves, crushed

600g diced beef

2 large carrots, diced

2 celery sticks, diced

400g tin chopped tomatoes

1 tbsp tomato purée

75ml beef stock

75ml red wine or more stock

½ tsp dried rosemary

½ tsp dried thyme

tagliatelle or other pasta, to serve

METHOD

1. Add all ingredients to the slow cooker and mix well.

2. Cook on high for 5-6 hours or low for 6-8 hours.

3. Serve with cooked tagliatelle.

STORING

Leftovers can be cooled and kept in a sealed container in the fridge for up to 2 days. Heat thoroughly in the microwave or on the hob before serving.

FREEZING

Freeze in containers or freezer bags for up to 3 months. Defrost in the fridge overnight and then reheat in the microwave or on the hob.

CAULIFLOWER MAC & CHEESE

| Serves: 4 | Prep time: 5 minutes | Cook time: 2–2.5 hours | Equipment: Slow cooker |

Sneak some cauliflower into this kid-friendly slow cooker mac & cheese for a tasty and nutritious family meal.

INGREDIENTS

150g finely diced cauliflower

900ml whole milk

100g cream cheese

100g grated Cheddar cheese

100g grated Red Leicester cheese

½ tsp smoked paprika

½ tsp garlic granules

400g macaroni

METHOD

1. The cauliflower for this recipe needs to be very finely diced. You can buy packs of frozen diced cauliflower which will work well here and can be added straight from the freezer. Or see page 161 for instructions on how to prep your own at home.

2. Add the milk, cream cheese, Cheddar, Red Leicester, paprika and garlic granules to the slow cooker and mix well.

3. Add the macaroni and cauliflower and then cook on high for 2–2.5 hours.

STORING

Leftovers can be cooled and kept in a sealed container in the fridge for up to 2 days. Heat thoroughly in the microwave or on the hob before serving.

FREEZING

Freeze in containers or freezer bags for up to 2 months. Defrost in the fridge overnight and then reheat in the microwave or on the hob.

VEGGIE BOLOGNESE

Fitting in some vegetarian meals mid-week is easy with this slow cooker bolognese.
It's packed with so much flavour that you won't even miss the meat!

INGREDIENTS

1 onion, diced

2 garlic cloves, crushed

3 carrots, diced

2 celery sticks, chopped

150g mushrooms, chopped

1 pepper, chopped

120g red lentils

400g tin chopped tomatoes

400ml vegetable stock

2 tbsp tomato purée

1 tbsp balsamic vinegar

½ tsp dried rosemary

½ tsp dried thyme

spaghetti, to serve

METHOD

1. Put all the ingredients in the slow cooker.

2. Cook on high for 4–5 hours or low for 5–6 hours.

3. This is optional, but once it's ready you can blitz the sauce to make it more kid-friendly. Simply cool slightly, then blitz with a hand blender or add to a stand blender.

4. Serve with cooked spaghetti.

STORING

Leftovers can be cooled and kept in a sealed container in the fridge for up to 2 days. Heat thoroughly in the microwave or on the hob before serving.

FREEZING

Freeze in containers or freezer bags for up to 3 months. Defrost in the fridge overnight and then reheat in the microwave or on the hob.

BEEF CASSEROLE

| Serves: 4 | Prep time: 10 minutes | Cook time: 4–6 hours | Equipment: Large frying pan and slow cooker |

This is my ultimate winter comfort food. If you are in a rush then feel free to skip the first step and not fry the beef, but if you have a few minutes to spare then it's worth doing as it really does help seal in the flavour.

INGREDIENTS

½ tbsp oil

500g diced beef

1 onion, diced

2 garlic cloves, crushed

3 carrots, diced

2 celery sticks, chopped

200ml beef stock

2 tbsp beef gravy granules

1 tbsp tomato purée

½ tsp dried rosemary

mashed potato, to serve

METHOD

1. Heat the oil in a large frying pan and add the beef. Cook for a few minutes until all sides have browned.

2. Add the beef to the slow cooker along with the rest of the ingredients and stir well.

3. Cook on high for 4-5 hours or low for 5-6 hours.

4. Serve with mashed potato.

STORING

Leftovers can be cooled and kept in a sealed container in the fridge for up to 2 days. Heat thoroughly in the microwave or on the hob before serving.

FREEZING

Freeze in containers or freezer bags for up to 3 months. Defrost in the fridge overnight and then reheat in the microwave or on the hob.

CHICKEN CASSEROLE

| Serves: 4 | Prep time: 6 minutes | Cook time: 4–6 hours | Equipment: Slow cooker |

This all-in-one casserole is ideal for the busiest of days. Everything gets cooked together in the slow cooker, including the potatoes, so there's no need to prep and cook any sides.

INGREDIENTS

500g baby potatoes

500g skinless chicken thighs

3 carrots, diced

1 onion, diced

2 garlic cloves, crushed

250ml chicken stock

2 tbsp chicken gravy granules

1 tbsp tomato purée

1 tsp French mustard

200g mushrooms

cooked green vegetables like broccoli or kale, to serve

METHOD

1. Chop the baby potatoes in half and add them to the slow cooker along with the rest of the ingredients, except for the mushrooms.

2. Stir well and then cook on high for 4–5 hours or low for 5–6 hours. Add the mushrooms halfway through cooking.

3. Serve with cooked green vegetables.

STORING

Leftovers can be cooled and kept in a sealed container in the fridge for up to 2 days. Heat thoroughly in the microwave or on the hob before serving.

FREEZING

Freeze in containers or freezer bags for up to 3 months. Defrost in the fridge overnight and then reheat in the microwave or on the hob.

SAUSAGE CASSEROLE

   NF

| Serves: 4 | Prep time: 2 minutes | Cook time: 4–6 hours | Equipment: Slow cooker |

This is another favourite of both my children. A simple sausage casserole slow cooked with vegetables and lentils.

INGREDIENTS

1 onion, sliced

2 garlic cloves, crushed

2 medium carrots, diced

1 celery stick, chopped

8 sausages, cut in half

400g tin chopped tomatoes

100g green lentils

250ml chicken stock

1 tbsp balsamic vinegar

1 tbsp honey

1 tsp smoked paprika

½ tsp dried rosemary

½ tsp dried thyme

100g frozen peas

crusty bread, to serve

METHOD

1. Add all the ingredients except the frozen peas to the slow cooker.

2. Cook on high for 4–5 hours or low for 5–6 hours.

3. Add the frozen peas for the last 15 minutes of cooking.

4. Serve with crusty bread.

STORING

Leftovers can be cooled and kept in a sealed container in the fridge for up to 2 days. Heat thoroughly in the microwave or on the hob before serving.

FREEZING

Freeze in containers or freezer bags for up to 3 months. Defrost in the fridge overnight and then reheat in the microwave or on the hob.

THAI POTATO CURRY

GF DF EF   NF V

If you ever find yourself with lots of new potatoes to use up, this curry is a must-try. The Thai curry paste adds bags of flavour and helps to make a really cheap and cheerful vegetarian dinner.

INGREDIENTS

1kg new potatoes

400ml tin coconut milk

4 tbsp Thai red curry paste

100ml water

400g tin cooked chickpeas

100g baby spinach

boiled rice or microwave rice, to serve

STORING

Leftovers can be cooled and kept in a sealed container in the fridge for up to 2 days. Heat thoroughly in the microwave or on the hob before serving.

FREEZING

Freeze in containers or freezer bags for up to 2 months. Defrost in the fridge overnight and then reheat in the microwave or on the hob.

METHOD

1. Leave the skins on the potatoes and cut them into bite-sized chunks.

2. Add the coconut milk, curry paste and water to the slow cooker and mix well.

3. Add the potatoes and then cook on high for 3 hours or low for 4 hours.

4. Drain the chickpeas and stir them in to the curry, then cook for another hour.

5. Check the potatoes are cooked through and then add spinach. It will wilt in the heat and doesn't need any extra cooking time.

6. Serve with rice.

COOK ONCE, EAT TWICE

One-Tray Roast Chicken Dinner
BBQ Chicken Tortilla Pizza

Sweet Potato & Paneer Curry
Paneer Curry Puffs

Hidden Veg Bolognese
Mini Bolognese Cups

Cheesy Leek Risotto
Baked Arancini

Garlic Butter Salmon & Potatoes
Creamy Salmon & Pea Pasta

Creamy Chicken & Mushrooms with Rice
Chicken Filo Pie

ONE-TRAY ROAST CHICKEN DINNER

| Serves: 4, plus leftovers | Prep time: 10 minutes | Cook time: 1 hour 35 minutes | Equipment: Large, deep roasting tin and large jug |

Love a Sunday roast but hate the faff involved in prepping all the ingredients, not to mention the washing up at the end? Try my One-Tray Roast Chicken Dinner recipe. All the delicious elements of a roast cooked in one tray!

INGREDIENTS

1 medium whole chicken

1 tbsp oil

1 chicken stock cube

500g new potatoes

4 medium carrots

2 parsnips

2 garlic cloves

600ml hot water

4 tbsp chicken gravy granules

200g tenderstem broccoli

LEFTOVERS

I find it easier to remove leftover chicken from the bone when it's completely cold. So I would recommend putting what is left of the whole chicken into a large bowl and keeping in the fridge overnight.

The following day, when you are ready to make your second meal from the chicken, it will be really easy to pick off the meat.

Once you've removed all the meat from the chicken you can use the carcass to make chicken stock (see page 156).

METHOD

1. Preheat the oven to 200°C/180°C Fan/ Gas Mark 6.

2. Put the chicken in a large deep roasting tin.

3. Rub the oil into the skin and crumble over the chicken stock cube. This will give a really crisp and tasty skin.

4. Cut the potatoes in half and add them to the tin.

5. Peel and chop the carrots and parsnips and add them too.

6. Peel the garlic but don't chop it. Crush with the back of the knife and add it to the tin whole.

7. Roast for 75 minutes, remove the tin from the oven and take out all the vegetables. Keep them to one side in a large bowl.

8. Mix the hot water and gravy granules in a jug until smooth and pour this into the tin around the chicken.

9. Add the tenderstem broccoli, making sure it's mostly covered in the gravy.

10. Return the tin to the oven for another 20 minutes.

11. Add the vegetables back to the tin for the last 5 minutes, mixing with the gravy and broccoli. This will heat them back up if they have gone a little cold.

12. Serve immediately.

BBQ CHICKEN TORTILLA PIZZA

| Serves: 4 | Prep time: 5 minutes | Cook time: 8 minutes | Equipment: Baking trays |

Use your leftover roast chicken to create this delicious smoky BBQ Chicken Pizza in less than 15 minutes.

INGREDIENTS

5 tbsp ketchup

1 tbsp honey

1 tbsp white wine vinegar

1 tbsp Worcestershire sauce

½ tsp smoked paprika

leftover chicken meat

4 large tortilla wraps

2 tbsp passata or pizza sauce

50g grated Cheddar cheese

salad or chopped crudités, to serve

METHOD

1. Preheat the oven to 200°C/180°C Fan/ Gas Mark 6 and line 2 baking trays with parchment paper.

2. Make the BBQ sauce by mixing the ketchup, honey, white wine vinegar, Worcestershire sauce and smoked paprika together in a bowl.

3. Add the leftover chicken and mix well.

4. Place 2 tortilla wraps on each of the trays.

5. Spread a thin layer of passata or pizza sauce over them.

6. Sprinkle on some grated cheese and place the BBQ chicken on top.

7. Bake in the oven for 7–8 minutes until the cheese is bubbling and the base is getting crispy.

8. Serve with salad or chopped crudités.

SWEET POTATO & PANEER CURRY

| Serves: 4, plus leftovers | Prep time: 7 minutes | Cook time: 25 minutes | Equipment: Large frying pan or shallow casserole dish |

This delicious vegetarian curry is a really tasty alternative to a classic chicken curry. It's mild in spice but can easily be jazzed up at the end for the adults with a splash of chilli sauce.

INGREDIENTS

750g sweet potato

½ tbsp oil

1 onion, diced

2 garlic cloves, crushed

3 tsp chopped ginger

1 ½ tsp garam masala

1 tsp mild chilli powder

1 ½ x 400g tins chopped tomatoes

600ml vegetable stock

300g paneer

150ml single cream

1 tbsp butter

boiled rice or microwave rice, to serve

METHOD

1. Peel the sweet potato and cut into 2cm chunks.

2. Put the oil, onion, garlic and ginger in a large frying pan or shallow casserole dish and cook for 2-3 minutes on medium heat.

3. Add the garam masala and chilli powder and cook for another minute, stirring continuously.

4. Add chopped tomatoes, vegetable stock and sweet potato. Bring to the boil and simmer for about 15 minutes until the potato is cooked.

5. In the meantime, dice the paneer.

6. Stir in the cream and butter and then add the paneer.

7. Cook for a further 5 minutes until the cheese has warmed through.

8. Serve with rice.

LEFTOVERS

This recipe will make enough for a family of 4, plus leftovers to make Paneer Curry Puffs (see page 120).

Place the leftover curry in a container and store in the fridge for up to 2 days.

PANEER CURRY PUFFS

| Makes: 6 | Prep time: 10 minutes | Cook time: 20 minutes | Equipment: Baking tray |

Turn your leftover curry into something completely different for dinner the following day using just a sheet of puff pastry.

INGREDIENTS

Leftover Sweet Potato and Paneer Curry

1 sheet ready-rolled puff pastry

1 egg or 1 tbsp milk (dairy or non-dairy)

salad and chopped veggies, to serve

METHOD

1. Preheat the oven to 220°C/200°C Fan/ Gas Mark 7 and line a baking tray with parchment paper.

2. Use a knife to cut the sweet potato and paneer a little smaller in the sauce. This will make it easier to fill and close the pastry parcels.

3. Unroll the pastry and cut into 6 even squares.

4. Put a large spoonful of the curry in the centre of the pastry.

5. Take the bottom-right corner of the pastry and fold it over the curry to meet the top-left corner of the pasty, making a triangle shape.

6. Seal the open edges with a fork and transfer the parcel to the baking tray.

7. Repeat with the remaining pastry squares.

8. Brush with a little beaten egg or milk, pierce the top with a fork and then bake in the oven for 20 minutes.

9. Allow to cool for a few minutes on a wire rack before serving.

10. Serve with salad or chopped veggies.

HIDDEN VEG BOLOGNESE

| Serves: 4, plus leftovers | Prep time: 12 minutes | Cook time: 40 minutes | Equipment: Large pan or shallow casserole dish |

Spaghetti bolognese is always a family favourite. Boost the nutritional value of this classic recipe with hidden carrot, courgette, peppers and leeks. Great for fussy eaters!

INGREDIENTS

2 carrots

1 courgette

1 red pepper

1 leek

1 tbsp oil

1 onion, diced

2 garlic cloves, crushed

750g minced beef (or veggie equivalent)

600g tinned chopped tomatoes

450ml beef stock

200ml red wine or more stock

3 tbsp tomato purée

2 tbsp balsamic vinegar

1 tsp dried oregano

spaghetti, to serve

METHOD

1. Prepare all the vegetables first. Peel the carrots and grate them. Grate the courgette and then chop the red pepper and leek very finely.

2. Heat the oil in a large pan or shallow casserole dish.

3. Add the onion, garlic and vegetables and cook for 3-4 minutes.

4. Add the minced beef (or veggie equivalent) and continue to fry for another 4 minutes until browned.

5. Add the chopped tomatoes, stock, red wine (if using), tomato purée, balsamic vinegar and dried oregano.

6. Bring to the boil and then simmer on high for 25-30 minutes.

7. Serve with cooked spaghetti.

LEFTOVERS

This recipe will make enough for a family of 4, plus leftovers to make Mini Bolognese Cups (see page 123).

Place the leftover bolognese in a container and store in the fridge for up to 2 days.

MINI BOLOGNESE CUPS

| Serves: 4 | Prep time: 15 minutes | Cook time: 15 minutes | Equipment: Muffin tray |

Take leftover bolognese and use it to make a tasty filling for these Mini Bolognese Cups the following day.

INGREDIENTS

butter or oil for greasing

3 large tortilla wraps

leftover Hidden Veg Bolognese

80g grated Cheddar cheese

salad, to serve

METHOD

1. Preheat the oven to 200°C/180°C Fan/ Gas Mark 6 and grease a 12-hole muffin tray with melted butter or oil. We will only be using 8 of the muffin holes.

2. Use a 10cm round pastry cutter or bowl to cut out 8 circles from the tortilla wraps.

3. Press the tortilla circles down into the muffin holes.

4. Add a large spoonful of the bolognese to the tortilla cup and top with a little grated cheese.

5. Bake in the oven for 12–15 minutes until the bolognese is heated throughout.

6. Serve with a salad.

CHEESY LEEK RISOTTO

| Serves: 4, plus leftovers | Prep time: 4 minutes | Cook time: 45 minutes | Equipment: Large frying pan or shallow casserole dish |

This risotto recipe couldn't be any easier to make. It's all baked in the oven meaning you don't have to stand over the stove adding stock and stirring. So simple!

INGREDIENTS

1 tbsp oil

1 onion, diced

2 garlic cloves, crushed

2 medium leeks, finely diced

450g risotto rice

1.8 litres hot vegetable stock

1 tsp dried thyme

75g grated Cheddar cheese

50g grated Parmesan

1 tbsp butter

salad, to serve

METHOD

1. Preheat the oven to 200°C/180°C Fan/ Gas Mark 6.

2. Add the oil, onion, garlic and leeks to a large shallow casserole dish and bake for 5 minutes.

3. Add the rice, stock and thyme and cook for 30-40 minutes until the stock has absorbed and the rice is cooked, stirring a few times.

4. Add more stock to the dish if you think it's getting too dry at any stage.

5. Stir in the Cheddar, Parmesan and butter and mix well.

6. Serve with salad.

LEFTOVERS

This recipe will make enough for a family of 4, plus leftovers to make Baked Arancini (see page 126).

Cool the leftover risotto quickly and place in a container. Store in the fridge for up to 2 days.

BAKED ARANCINI

| Serves: 4 | Prep time: 15 minutes | Cook time: 30 minutes | Equipment: Baking tray |

Turn leftover risotto into delicious baked rice balls for a completely new
and fun dinner the next day.

INGREDIENTS

30g plain flour

2 eggs

80g panko breadcrumbs

leftover Cheesy Leek Risotto

1 tbsp oil

side salad or crudités, to serve

METHOD

1. Preheat the oven to 220°C/200°C Fan/
    Gas Mark 7 and line a baking tray with
    parchment paper.

2. Put the flour in one bowl. Crack the eggs into a
    second bowl and whisk gently with a fork.

3. Then add the panko breadcrumbs to a third bowl.

4. Take about 2 heaped tablespoons of the leftover
    risotto, roll it with your hands into a ball. Roll it
    in the flour, dip in the egg and then coat in the
    panko breadcrumbs.

5. Place on the baking tray and then repeat with the
    rest of the risotto.

6. When they're ready to cook brush the top of the
    rice balls with a little oil, then bake in the oven
    for 25-30 minutes until golden brown and heated
    through.

7. Serve with salad or crudités.

GARLIC BUTTER SALMON & POTATOES

| Serves: 4, plus leftovers | Prep time: 6 minutes | Cook time: 25 minutes | Equipment: Two baking trays or dishes |

Fish can be very expensive to buy fresh. For my next two recipes I use frozen salmon fillets. Much cheaper to buy and they have already removed the skin too.

INGREDIENTS

6 frozen salmon fillets

50g butter

3 garlic cloves, crushed

6 sprigs of fresh dill

salt and pepper

700g baby potatoes

1 tbsp oil

salad or cooked green vegetables like broccoli or kale, to serve

LEFTOVERS

This recipe will make enough for a family of 4 plus leftovers to make Creamy Salmon & Pea Pasta (see page 130).

Place the two leftover salmon fillets plus any juice or garlic butter into a fridge for up to 2 days.

METHOD

1. Preheat the oven to 200°C/180°C Fan/ Gas Mark 6 and have 2 baking trays ready.

2. Line 1 tray with tin foil, scrunching the edges together to create a parcel for the salmon and garlic butter.

3. Add the frozen salmon fillets to the foil, topped with the butter, garlic and dill.

4. Season with a little salt and pepper.

5. Cut the baby potatoes in half and add to another tray, drizzling the oil on top.

6. Put both trays in the oven and cook for 25 minutes, checking that the salmon is cooked through and the potatoes are soft.

7. Serve with salad or cooked green veg.

CREAMY SALMON & PEA PASTA

| Serves: 4 | Prep time: 2 minutes | Cook time: 14 minutes | Equipment: Saucepan, large frying pan or shallow casserole dish |

Just two cooked leftover salmon fillets is enough to create this tasty salmon pasta meal the following day.

INGREDIENTS

350g pasta

250g crème fraîche

100g frozen peas

1 vegetable stock cube

2 leftover salmon fillets, broken up

2 sprigs of fresh dill

METHOD

1. Add the pasta to a saucepan and cook accordingly to the packet instructions.

2. Put the crème fraîche, frozen peas, vegetable stock cube and leftover salmon fillets in a large frying pan or shallow casserole dish and cook on low for about 5-6 minutes until the peas are cooked and the salmon has warmed through.

3. Drain the pasta, reserving a little of the pasta water.

4. Add the drained pasta to the frying pan and mix well. Add a splash of pasta water at a time until you get a nice sauce consistency.

5. Serve immediately with a little chopped dill on top.

CREAMY CHICKEN & MUSHROOMS WITH RICE

| Serves: 4, plus leftovers | Prep time: 5 minutes | Cook time: 25 minutes | Equipment: Large frying pan or shallow casserole dish |

Creamy chicken and mushrooms all cooked together in one pot. Delicious served with rice. Use microwave rice if you're short on time, or else boiled rice.

INGREDIENTS

1 tbsp oil

600g diced chicken breast

1 onion, diced

2 garlic cloves, crushed

3 medium leeks, finely diced

300g mushroom, roughly chopped

3 tbsp flour

450ml hot chicken stock

2 tsp French mustard

150ml single cream

boiled rice or microwave rice, to serve

LEFTOVERS

This recipe will make enough for a family of 4 plus leftovers to make Chicken Filo Pie (see page 133).

Place the leftover chicken & mushroom in a container and store in the fridge for up to 2 days.

METHOD

1. Add the oil and chicken to a large frying pan or shallow casserole dish.

2. Cook for 5-6 minutes until the chicken has browned, then remove the chicken from the pan.

3. Add the onion, garlic, leeks and mushrooms and cook for about 4 minutes until the veggies are softening.

4. Add the flour and stir quickly, cooking for 30 seconds.

5. Slowly add the hot chicken stock, stirring continuously until the lumps have all disappeared.

6. Add the chicken back to the pan along with the French mustard.

7. Bring to the boil and simmer for 10 minutes until the sauce has thickened.

8. Turn off the heat and stir in the cream.

9. Serve with rice.

CHICKEN FILO PIE

| Serves: 4 | Prep time: 10 minutes | Cook time: 25 minutes | Equipment: Pie dish |

Take the leftover Creamy Chicken & Mushrooms recipe and use it as a filling
for a delicious filo pie.

INGREDIENTS

leftover Creamy Chicken &
Mushrooms

100g frozen peas

200g pack filo pastry

2 tbsp butter

cooked green vegetables like
broccoli or kale, to serve

METHOD

1. Preheat the oven to 220°C/200°C Fan/
   Gas Mark 7.

2. Pour the leftover Creamy Chicken & Mushrooms
   directly into the pie dish, along with the frozen
   peas and mix well.

3. Unwrap the filo pastry and scrunch each sheet up
   in your hand, one at a time, then place on top of
   the pie filling. There's no right or wrong way to do
   this. Filo pastry is supposed to be messy!

4. Once you have filled the pie dish with the pastry,
   melt the butter and brush this over the top.

5. Bake in the oven for 20-25 minutes until the
   pastry is golden brown and the pie filling is
   piping hot.

6. Serve with cooked green veg.

FREEZER STASH BAGS

Spanish Chicken Stew
Thai Honey Garlic Chicken Wraps
Steak Fajitas
Chicken Tikka Masala
Meatball Minestrone Soup
Greek Lamb & Orzo Casserole
Chunky Vegetable Soup
Freezer Fried Rice

SPANISH CHICKEN STEW

| Serves: 4 | Prep time: 7 minutes | Cook time: 1 hour in oven. 4–6 hours in slow cooker | Equipment: Shallow casserole dish or slow cooker |

This delicious Spanish-flavoured stew is more summery than a traditional stew. You can also swap the chicken thighs for chicken breasts if you prefer.

INGREDIENTS

600g skinless chicken thighs, left whole

100g chorizo, chopped

2 peppers, chopped

400g tin chopped tomatoes

400g tin cannellini or butter beans

2 garlic cloves, crushed

50g pitted olives

2 tbsp olive oil

1 tbsp white wine vinegar

1 tsp smoked paprika

½ tsp dried rosemary

crusty bread for dipping

METHOD

1. Add all the ingredients to a large freezer bag. Push out the air and seal the bag.

2. Freeze flat for up to 3 months.

3. Defrost in a large bowl in the fridge overnight and then cook either in the oven or slow cooker.

4. Serve with crusty bread.

OVEN

Add the contents of the bag to a large oven dish. Add 400ml of hot chicken stock and cook at 200°C/180°C Fan/Gas Mark 6 for 1 hour, stirring a few times.

SLOW COOKER

Add the contents of the bag to the slow cooker along with 200ml of hot chicken stock. Cook on high for 4-5 hours or low for 5-6 hours.

THAI HONEY GARLIC CHICKEN WRAPS

| Serves: 4 | Prep time: 5 minutes | Cook time: 35 minutes in oven. 4–6 hours in slow cooker | Equipment: Large oven dish or slow cooker |

Slow-cook these marinated chicken breasts in the oven or slow cooker to make the meat super tender and perfect to add to wraps.

INGREDIENTS

4 chicken breasts

1 tbsp Thai Red Curry Paste

3 garlic cloves, crushed

3 tbsp honey

2 tbsp soy sauce

1 tbsp tomato purée

juice of 1 lime

100ml water

1 tsp cornflour

tortilla wraps and salad, to serve

METHOD

1. Put all the ingredients except the water and cornflour into a large freezer bag.

2. Combine water and cornflour in a cup and stir until dissolved.

3. Pour this into the bag and mix well. Push out the air and seal the bag.

4. Freeze flat for up to 3 months.

5. Defrost in a large bowl in the fridge overnight and then cook either in the oven or slow cooker.

6. Serve with tortilla wraps and salad.

OVEN

Put the contents of the bag into a large oven dish. Cook at 200°C/180°C Fan/Gas Mark 6 for 35–40 minutes, checking to ensure that the chicken breasts are piping hot and cooked through. Shred the chicken with two forks.

SLOW COOKER

Put the contents of the bag into the slow cooker. Cook on high for 4–5 hours or low for 5–6 hours. Shred the chicken with two forks.

STEAK FAJITAS

| Serves: 4 | Prep time: 5 minutes | Cook time: 12 minutes | Equipment: Large frying pan |

You can't beat sizzling fajitas for a quick and easy mid-week meal. And you can make it even easier by prepping all the ingredients in advance. This also gives the beef a chance to marinade in all the spices and lime juice.

INGREDIENTS

350g beef steaks, sliced

1 red onion, chopped

3 peppers, sliced

juice of 1 lime

1 tsp ground cumin

1 tsp smoked paprika

½ tsp mild chilli powder

½ tsp garlic powder

tortilla wraps, guacamole, sour cream, salsa, coriander and grated cheese, to serve

METHOD

1. Put all the ingredients into a large freezer bag. Push out the air and seal the bag.

2. Freeze flat for up to 3 months.

3. Defrost in a large bowl in the fridge overnight and then add the contents of the bag to a large frying pan along with a little oil.

4. Fry for 10-12 minutes until the beef has cooked and the vegetables have softened.

5. Serve with tortilla wraps and all your favourite toppings.

See Steak Fajitas image overleaf

CHICKEN TIKKA MASALA

| Serves: 4 | Prep time: 5 minutes | Cook time: 50 minutes in oven. 4–6 hours in slow cooker | Equipment: Shallow casserole dish or slow cooker |

The easiest chicken curry recipe you will ever make. Prep the ingredients ahead of time and all you need to do is pop them into the oven or slow cooker for a delicious creamy Chicken Tikka Masala dinner.

INGREDIENTS

1 onion, diced

2 garlic cloves, crushed

1 tsp chopped ginger

2 tsp garam masala

1 tbsp mild curry powder

1 tbsp mango chutney

400g tin chopped tomatoes

2 tbsp tomato purée

400ml tin coconut milk

600g diced chicken breast

boiled or microwave rice, to serve

METHOD

1. Put all ingredients except chicken into a large freezer bag. Mix well with a spoon and then add chicken.

2. Push out the air from the bag and then seal.

3. Freeze flat for up to 3 months.

4. Defrost in a large bowl in the fridge overnight and then cook either in the oven or slow cooker.

5. Serve with boiled rice.

OVEN

Add the contents of the bag to a large oven dish and cook at 200°C/180°C Fan/Gas Mark 6 for 50 minutes, stirring a few times.

SLOW COOKER

Add the contents of the bag to the slow cooker. Cook on high for 4-5 hours or low for 5-6 hours.

MEATBALL MINESTRONE SOUP

| Serves: 4 | Prep time: 8 minutes | Cook time: 20 minutes on the hob. 3–5 hours in the slow cooker | Equipment: Large saucepan or slow cooker |

This is the ultimate comfort food to serve up on a cold winter's evening to your hungry brood. It's hearty and filling and very kid-friendly too.

INGREDIENTS

1 onion, diced

2 garlic cloves, crushed

2 carrots, diced

1 celery stick, chopped

2 x 400g tins chopped tomatoes

2 tbsp tomato purée

125g pasta (macaroni or another small pasta shape)

1 tsp dried oregano

12 beef meatballs

crusty bread for dipping

METHOD

1. Put all the ingredients except the meatballs into a large freezer bag. Mix well with a spoon and then add the meatballs.

2. Push out the air from the bag and then seal.

3. Freeze flat for up to 3 months.

4. Defrost in a large bowl in the fridge overnight and then cook either on the hob or slow cooker.

5. Serve with crusty bread.

HOB

Add the contents of the bag to a large saucepan. Add 1 litre of hot vegetable stock, bring to the boil and then cook on a simmer for 20 minutes.

SLOW COOKER

Add the contents of the bag to the slow cooker along with 1 litre of hot vegetable stock. Cook on high for 3 hours or low for 4–5 hours.

GREEK LAMB & ORZO CASSEROLE

Serves: 4 | Prep time: 7 minutes | Cook time: 1 hour in the oven. 4–6 hours in the slow cooker | Equipment: Shallow casserole dish or slow cooker |

An easy and tasty all-in-one Mediterranean casserole. A great way to introduce children to new flavours.

INGREDIENTS

400g diced lamb

250g orzo

1 red onion, diced

2 garlic cloves, crushed

2 carrots, diced

400g tin chopped tomatoes

50g pitted olives

1 tbsp honey

1 tsp dried oregano

1 tsp smoked paprika

¼ tsp cinnamon

75g feta, to serve

METHOD

1. Put all the ingredients into a large freezer bag. Push out the air and seal the bag.

2. Freeze flat for up to 3 months.

3. Defrost in a large bowl in the fridge overnight and then cook either in the oven or slow cooker.

4. Serve with crumbled feta on top.

OVEN

Put the contents of the bag into a large oven dish along with 1 litre of lamb or beef stock. Cook at 200°C/180°C Fan/Gas Mark 6 for 1 hour, stirring a few times.

SLOW COOKER

Put the contents of the bag into the slow cooker. Add 500ml of lamb or beef stock and cook on high for 4–5 hours or low for 5–6 hours, adding some extra stock if you need it.

CHUNKY VEGETABLE SOUP

| Serves: 4 | Prep time: 7 minutes | Cook time: 15 minutes on the hob. 3–4 hours in the slow cooker | Equipment: Large saucepan or slow cooker |

This Chunky Vegetable Soup is super-filling and ideal for a warming lunch or dinner. It's the only Freezer Stash Bag that can be cooked directly from frozen, making it ideal to pull out of the freezer on a whim!

INGREDIENTS

3 medium carrots, diced

2 celery sticks, chopped

2 garlic cloves, crushed

1 leek, chopped

100g green beans (fresh or frozen)

400g tin cannellini or butter beans

2 tbsp pesto

1 tsp dried oregano

METHOD

1. Put all the ingredients into a large freezer bag. Push out the air and seal bag.

2. Freeze flat for up to 2 months.

3. This soup can be cooked from frozen either on the hob or the slow cooker.

HOB

Put the contents of the bag into a large saucepan along with 1.5 litres of hot vegetable stock.

Bring to the boil, reduce to a simmer and cook for 15 minutes until the vegetable are soft.

SLOW COOKER

Put the contents of the bag into the slow cooker along with 1.5 litres of hot vegetable stock. Cook on high for 3 hours or low for 4 hours.

FREEZER FRIED RICE

| Serves: 4 | Prep time: 15 minutes | Cook time: 15 minutes | Equipment: Large saucepan and wok or large frying pan |

These rice bags are brilliant to prep ahead and have on hand for busy mid-week meals. You can add protein to the rice such as frozen prawns or cooked chicken or ham.

INGREDIENTS

250g easy-cook long-grain rice

250g chopped frozen vegetables

1 pepper, chopped

2 spring onions, chopped

2 garlic cloves, crushed

To cook:

2 tbsp sesame oil

2 eggs

1 tbsp soy sauce

METHOD

1. Cook the rice according to the packet instructions.

2. Once cooked, cool it as quickly as possible. I do this by spreading it out on a large plate or tray.

3. Once cooled, add the rice to a large freezer bag along with the chopped frozen vegetables, peppers, spring onions and garlic.

4. Push out the air and then seal the bag.

5. Freeze flat for up to 2 months.

6. Defrost in the fridge overnight.

7. Heat the sesame oil in a wok or large frying pan.

8. Add the contents of the bag to the wok or large frying pan.

9. Cook for 8–10 minutes until the rice is piping hot, stirring regularly.

10. Make a well in the middle of the wok or pan and crack in the eggs.

11. Mix the eggs with a spatula but try to keep the rice out of the eggs at this stage.

12. Cook for a couple of minutes until they resemble scrambled eggs and then mix with the rice.

13. Add the soy sauce and stir again.

STOCK, SIDES & SAUCES

Everyday Tomato Sauce
No-Cook Red Pesto
No-Cook Green Pesto
Chicken Stock
Vegetable Stock
Freezer Roast Potatoes
Cheddar & Chive Mash
Sneaky Diced Cauliflower
Bottom of the Fridge Ratatouille

EVERYDAY TOMATO SAUCE

| Serves: 4 | Prep time: 5 minutes | Cook time: 35 minutes | Equipment: Large saucepan |

This basic tomato sauce recipe is a staple in my house. I always have a batch in the freezer ready to turn into a delicious family meal. Use it as a simple pasta sauce or mix it with some mascarpone for something a bit more luxurious. You can also use it for pizzas or pour over chicken breasts and bake in the oven.

INGREDIENTS

1 tbsp oil

1 onion, finely diced

2 cloves garlic, crushed

2 x 400g tins chopped tomatoes

300ml vegetable stock

4 tbsp tomato purée

2 tbsp balsamic vinegar

1 tsp sugar

1 tsp dried basil

½ tsp dried oregano

METHOD

1. Heat the oil in a large saucepan and add the onions and garlic. Sauté for about 3 minutes until the onions have softened.

2. Add the rest of the ingredients, bring to the boil and then reduce to a low simmer for 30 minutes.

3. You can serve the sauce as it is or blitz it to make it completely smooth.

STORING

This sauce will keep in an airtight container in the fridge for up to 2 days.

FREEZING

Freeze in bags or containers. Defrost overnight in the fridge and reheat on the hob or in the microwave.

NO-COOK RED PESTO

| Serves: 8 | Prep time: 5 minutes | Cook time: NA | Equipment: Stand blender or smoothie maker |

This is the recipe you need in your life when you literally have 10 minutes to get dinner on the table! In less time than it takes to cook a pan of pasta you can make this delicious No-Cook Red Pesto Sauce that the whole family will love, with loads left over to freeze for another day.

INGREDIENTS

200g roasted red peppers
(from a jar)

100g sun-dried tomatoes

150g light olive oil

70g grated Parmesan

juice of ½ lemon

¼ clove of garlic

METHOD

1. Add all the ingredients to a blender or smoothie maker and blitz until smooth.

2. Serve as a pasta sauce or a sauce for chicken or fish.

STORING

This sauce will keep in an airtight container in the fridge for up to 2 days.

FREEZING

You can freeze this sauce in bags or containers for up to 3 months and defrost in the fridge overnight. You can also freeze smaller individual portions in pots/ice cube trays. These will defrost a lot quicker.

Reheat the sauce on the hob until piping hot.

NO-COOK GREEN PESTO

| Serves: 8 | Prep time: 5 minutes | Cook time: NA | Equipment: Stand blender or smoothie maker |

If you prefer the more classic green pesto then try my version that contains some sneaky spinach. Great for the picky eaters in your family!

INGREDIENTS

50g baby spinach

25g fresh basil

60g pine nuts

200ml light olive oil

70g grated Parmesan

juice of ½ lemon

¼ clove of garlic

METHOD

1. Add all the ingredients to a blender or smoothie maker and blitz until smooth.

2. Serve as a pasta sauce or a sauce for chicken or fish.

STORING

This sauce will keep in an airtight container in the fridge for up to 2 days.

FREEZING

You can freeze this sauce in bags or containers for up to 3 months and defrost in the fridge overnight. You can also freeze smaller individual portions in pots/ice cube trays. These will defrost a lot quicker.

Reheat the sauce on the hob until piping hot.

CHICKEN STOCK

| Serves: 4 | Prep time: 3 minutes | Cook time: 2 hours 10 minutes | Equipment: Very large saucepan or stock pot and large jug |

If you cook a whole roast chicken then it really is worth keeping the carcass and making your own homemade chicken stock the following day. It's probably a lot easier than you think and the result is well worth the effort.

INGREDIENTS

1 cooked chicken carcass

3 carrots

3 celery sticks

1 onion

4 garlic cloves

salt and pepper

STORING

This stock will keep in the fridge for up to 3 days.

FREEZING

You can freeze the stock in bags or containers for up to 3 months and defrost in the fridge overnight. You can also freeze smaller individual portions in pots/ice cube trays. These will defrost a lot quicker.

METHOD

1. Add the chicken carcass to a very large saucepan or stock pot.

2. Roughly chop the carrots, celery and onion. There is no need to peel these. Add to the pot.

3. Crush the garlic with the back of a knife but leave it whole. Add that to the pot.

4. Add 3 litres of cold water to the pot.

5. If your saucepan is not big enough then add less water to begin with. You can add more as it starts to evaporate and reduce in volume.

6. Bring to the boil and simmer for about 2 hours.

7. Pour the stock through a sieve into a large jug and season to taste with salt and pepper.

8. Leave to cool and skim off any fat from the top and store.

VEGETABLE STOCK

| Serves: 4 | Prep time: 1 minute | Cook time: 1 hour | Equipment: Large saucepan and large jug |

Keep the odds and ends of vegetables including trimmings and peelings and small amounts of fresh herbs too. Keep them in the freezer until you have enough to make your own delicious homemade vegetable stock.

INGREDIENTS

Odds and ends of vegetables and peelings, including:

onions

garlic

green tops of leeks

celery

carrots

spring onions

And herbs including:

bay

thyme

oregano

stalks of parsley and coriander

STORING

This stock will keep in the fridge for up to 5 days.

FREEZING

You can freeze the stock in bags or containers for up to 3 months and defrost in the fridge overnight. You can also freeze smaller individual portions in pots/ice cube trays. These will defrost a lot quicker.

METHOD

1. Save peelings from vegetables and scrappy ends as well as any stray bits of herbs or herb stalks. Keep a large bag in the freezer and keep adding to it until it is full.

2. When ready to make, add the contents of the bag to a large saucepan and cover with cold water.

3. Bring to the boil and simmer for about 1 hour.

4. Strain through a sieve into a large jug and store.

FREEZER ROAST POTATOES

| Serves: 4 | Prep time: 10 minutes | Cook time: 50 minutes | Equipment: Large saucepan and large baking tray |

Roast potatoes shouldn't be kept just for big Sunday roasts. Using my simple method you can have roast potatoes partially cooked and kept in the freezer, ready to be baked straight from frozen mid-week.

INGREDIENTS

1.2kg Maris Piper potatoes

3 tbsp oil

STORING

Roast potatoes are best eaten the day they are made but they can be kept in the fridge for up to 2 days and reheated in the oven or microwave.

FREEZING

To freeze, after Step 5 add the cooled potatoes to a large plate or tray and flash freeze for 1 hour. Transfer the potatoes to a freezer bag and keep in the freezer for up to 2 months.

Cook directly from frozen. Heat the oil in the baking tray as above and then add the frozen potatoes to it. Cook at 200°C/180°C Fan/Gas Mark 6 for 30 minutes and then 220°C/200°C Fan/Gas Mark 7 for another 30–45 minutes until cooked through and crispy. Do not be tempted to turn the potatoes, just leave them be!

METHOD

1. Peel the potatoes and chop them into halves or thirds, keeping the sizes as even as possible.

2. Add to a saucepan and cover with boiling water.

3. Simmer for 7 minutes.

4. Drain the potatoes well and leave them to cool for a few minutes in the colander.

5. Once the steam has stopped rising from the potatoes, shake them in the colander to bash the sides up a bit. This will help to make them extra crispy on the outside.

6. Meanwhile, heat the oven to 220°C/200°C Fan/Gas Mark 7 and add the oil to a large baking tray.

7. Put the baking tray in the oven whilst it is heating up to also heat the oil.

8. Once the oil is very hot, add the potatoes to the tray and coat them completely in the oil.

9. Bake in the oven for 35–40 minutes until cooked through and golden and crispy on the outside.

10. The key to all-over crispy roast potatoes is not to shake or turn them. Just leave them be in the tray!

11. Serve immediately.

CHEDDAR & CHIVE MASH

| Serves: 4 | Prep time: 10 minutes | Cook time: 18 minutes | Equipment: Large saucepan |

You can't beat a bowl of creamy mashed potato as the ultimate comfort side dish. Add a twist to this classic recipe with some grated Cheddar cheese and fresh chives. This is ideal to batch cook and have in the freezer for busy days.

INGREDIENTS

1.2kg Maris Piper potatoes

100ml milk

40g butter

100g grated Cheddar cheese

½ tbsp chopped chives

STORING

Mashed potatoes will keep in the fridge for up to 2 days. Reheat in the microwave or on the hob. You may need to add a splash more milk to it when reheating.

FREEZING

To freeze, put the mashed potato into a freezer bag. Once cool, place in the freezer and keep for up to 2 months

Defrost in the fridge overnight and then reheat in the microwave or on the hob. You may need to add a splash more milk to it when reheating.

METHOD

1. Peel the potatoes and chop them into equal-sized chunks.

2. Add to a saucepan and cover with boiling water.

3. Simmer for 12–15 minutes until soft.

4. Drain the potatoes well and add them back into the saucepan.

5. Add the milk and butter and mash with a potato masher until completely smooth.

6. Add the grated cheese and chives and mix well.

7. Serve immediately.

SNEAKY DICED CAULIFLOWER

 GF DF EF NF V

| Serves: 6 | Prep time: 6 minutes | Cook time: NA | Equipment: Food processor (but not essential) |

Diced cauliflower is so handy to have in the freezer ready to be added to lots of different recipes. This is brilliant for fussy eaters who normally would not touch cauliflower if served up whole!

INGREDIENTS

1 medium whole cauliflower

STORING

The blitzed cauliflower will keep in the fridge for 24 hours.

FREEZING

Add the blitzed cauliflower to a freezer bag and freeze for up to 2 months. It can be added direct from frozen to all recipes.

METHOD

1. Remove the green stalks from the cauliflower and cut off the majority of the stem.

2. Cut the rest into small florets. Add to a food processor and blitz. Be careful not to over-blitz the cauliflower. We want to break it down into the consistency of cous cous but not over-process it so that it starts to become mushy.

3. You can also do this with just a knife. Cut the florets up very finely. The result will be a little more chunky than if you use a food processor, but it works just fine.

4. Add the diced cauliflower to lots of recipes such as Creamy Banana Smoothie (see page 38), 3 Veg Mac & Cheese (see page 63) or Cauliflower Mac & Cheese (see page 104).

BOTTOM OF THE FRIDGE RATATOUILLE

| Serves: 4 | Prep time: 5 minutes | Cook time: 40 minutes | Equipment: Large saucepan and stand blender |

This recipe is ideal to use up any lingering vegetables at the bottom of the fridge that might be a little past their best. Turn them into a delicious side dish or even a hidden veggie pasta sauce for the kids.

INGREDIENTS

1 tbsp oil

1 onion, diced

2 garlic cloves, crushed

1 aubergine, chopped

1 courgette, chopped

1 pepper, chopped

250g tomatoes, chopped

400g tin chopped tomatoes

400ml water

1 tbsp balsamic vinegar

1 tsp sugar

10 basil leaves or 2 tsp dried basil

METHOD

1. Put the oil, onion and garlic into a large saucepan or frying pan on the hob and sauté for about 3 minutes until the onion starts to soften.

2. Add the aubergine, courgette, pepper and tomatoes and cook for another 4 minutes.

3. Add the tinned tomatoes, water, balsamic vinegar, sugar and basil and bring to the boil.

4. Simmer for 30 minutes.

5. Serve immediately as a side dish or blitz in a stand blender to break it down into a sauce. This is ideal to serve as a pasta sauce for kids.

STORING

This ratatouille can be kept in an airtight container in the fridge for up to 3 days.

FREEZING

Add to a freezer bag or container and freeze for up to 3 months. Defrost in the fridge overnight and reheat on the hob or in the microwave.

BIG BATCH SNACKS

Chocolate Peanut Butter Flapjacks
Carrot & Apple Cookies
No-Bake Chocolate Cookies
Chocolate Courgette Loaf
Strawberry Cream Cheese Muffins
Nut-Free Granola Bars
Bounty Energy Bites
Popcorn Bars
Apple Pie Wraps
Big Batch Brownie Mix
Fruit & Veg Fridge Packs
Chocolate Orange Brownie Cookies

CHOCOLATE PEANUT BUTTER FLAPJACKS

Makes: 9 | Prep time: 10 minutes | Cook time: 20 minutes, plus 15 minutes in the freezer | Equipment: Baking dish, large mixing bowl and large jug |

These flapjacks taste super decadent but are packed full of nutritious and filling ingredients. Ideal for a substantial afternoon snack for hungry kids!

INGREDIENTS

200g oats

100g smooth peanut butter

50g coconut oil or butter

50g honey

60g crunchy peanut butter

50g dark chocolate

STORING

Store the flapjacks in the fridge for 4-5 days.

FREEZING

Place the flapjacks on a tray or plate and flash freeze for an hour until hard. Transfer to a freezer bag or container for up to 3 months. Defrost at room temperature in 1 hour.

METHOD

1. Preheat the oven to 200°C/180°C Fan/ Gas Mark 6 and line a 20cm square baking dish with parchment paper.

2. Put the oats in a large bowl.

3. Put the smooth peanut butter, coconut oil or butter and honey in a large jug and melt in the microwave.

4. Pour this mixture into the oats and mix well.

5. Transfer to the dish and press down with the back of a spoon to make the mixture as compact as possible.

6. Bake for 20 mins. When you remove the dish from the oven, leave it to cool for a few minutes.

7. Melt the crunchy peanut butter and dark chocolate in a small jug in the microwave and then spread this mixture on top of the flapjacks.

8. Put the dish in the freezer for 15 minutes. This step is important as it allows you to cut the flapjacks without them crumbling.

9. Remove the flapjacks from the dish and cut into 9 squares.

CARROT & APPLE COOKIES

| Makes: 15 | Prep time: 15 minutes | Cook time: 20 minutes | Equipment: Baking trays, large mixing bowl and electric mixer |

Low in sugar but packed full of flavour, these cookies are ideal to batch make and pop from the freezer straight into lunch boxes.

INGREDIENTS

120g butter

50g light brown sugar

1 tsp vanilla extract

100g plain flour

100g oats

¼ tsp bicarbonate of soda

1 medium apple

1 medium carrot

STORING

Store the cookies in a tin or container for up to 2 days.

FREEZE

Place the cookies on a tray or plate and flash freeze for 1 hour until hard. Transfer to a freezer bag or container for up to 3 months. Defrost at room temperature in 2 hours.

METHOD

1. Preheat the oven to 200°C/180°C Fan/ Gas Mark 6 and line 2 baking trays with parchment paper.

2. In a large bowl cream together the butter, sugar and vanilla extract with an electric mixer.

3. Add the flour, oats and bicarbonate of soda and mix well with a spoon.

4. Grate the apple and carrot onto a plate. Squeeze out as much of the juice as possible. The juice will prevent the cookies from crisping up.

5. Add the grated apple and carrot to the cookie mixture and mix again.

6. Roll the mixture into 15 small cookies, dividing between the 2 trays.

7. Bake in the oven for 18–20 minutes.

8. Allow to cool on the tray for a few minutes (this is really important as the cookies will still be really soft) before moving to a wire rack to cool completely.

NO-BAKE CHOCOLATE COOKIES

| Makes: 12 | Prep time: 10 minutes, plus 1 hour in the fridge or freezer | Cook time: NA | Equipment: Baking tray, large mixing bowl and large jug |

All the taste of delicious crispy chocolate cookies but no cooking or baking required. These are brilliant to get kids involved in the kitchen.

INGREDIENTS

100g oats

20g puffed rice cereal, like Rice Krispies

125g peanut butter

50g coconut oil or butter

3 tbsp honey

2 tbsp cocoa powder

STORING

These cookies will keep in the fridge for 4 days.

FREEZING

Place the cookies on a tray or plate and flash freeze for 1 hour until hard. Transfer to a freezer bag or container for up to 3 months. Defrost at room temperature in 30 minutes.

METHOD

1. Line a baking tray or large plate with parchment paper. Just make sure it will fit in the fridge or freezer.

2. Pour the oats and cereal into a large bowl and mix.

3. Put the peanut butter, coconut oil or butter and honey in a jug and melt in the microwave.

4. Add the cocoa powder to this melted mixture, stirring well, then pour into the bowl of oats and cereal.

5. Mix everything quickly.

6. Take a spoonful of the mixture and place on the tray, forming into a round cookie shape.

7. Repeat with the rest of the mixture, making about 12 cookies.

8. Put the tray into the fridge or freezer for 1 hour to allow the cookies to firm up.

CHOCOLATE COURGETTE LOAF

| Makes: 12 slices | Prep time: 10 minutes | Cook time: 50 minutes | Equipment: Loaf tin, large mixing bowl and large jug |

A delicious soft chocolate loaf, sweetened with honey and banana, and a sneaky vegetable hidden too! Perfect to slice and freeze for snacks all week long.

INGREDIENTS

1 medium courgette

300g plain flour

1 tsp baking powder

¾ tsp bicarbonate of soda

2 tbsp cocoa powder

100g melted butter

75g honey

75g plain yoghurt

1 medium banana, mashed (or 80g apple sauce)

1 egg

50g chocolate chips

STORING

This loaf will keep in an airtight container for up to 3 days.

FREEZING

Freeze slices individually, wrapped in tin foil or parchment paper for up to 3 months. To defrost, leave at room temperature for 2-3 hours.

METHOD

1. Preheat the oven to 200°C/180°C Fan/ Gas Mark 6 and line a 900g (2lb) loaf tin with parchment paper.

2. Wash the courgette and finely grate it onto a plate. Set aside for the moment.

3. Put the flour, baking powder, bicarbonate of soda and cocoa powder in a large bowl and combine with a spoon.

4. In a jug or another bowl add the melted butter, honey, yoghurt, mashed banana and egg and mix well.

5. Pour the wet ingredients into the dry ingredients and mix well.

6. Squeeze the grated courgette to remove as much liquid as possible and add this to the mixture.

7. Finally, stir in the chocolate chips.

8. Transfer this mixture into the lined loaf tin and bake for 30 minutes.

9. Remove the tin from the oven and cover the top loosely with tin foil. This will stop the top of the cake from burning.

10. Bake for a further 20 minutes.

11. Allow the loaf to cool for a few minutes in the tin before turning out onto a wire rack and leaving it to cool further.

12. Cut into 12 slices (this loaf will be much easier to cut once it's cool).

STRAWBERRY CREAM CHEESE MUFFINS

| Makes: 12 | Prep time: 10 minutes | Cook time: 20 minutes | Equipment: Muffin tray, large mixing bowl and large jug |

Delicious fruity muffins made with cream cheese. Perfect to bake in bulk and pop into the freezer for snacks for weeks to come.

INGREDIENTS

300g plain flour

2 tsp baking powder

75g butter or coconut oil

2 eggs

150g cream cheese

100ml milk

80g honey

1 tsp vanilla

125g fresh or frozen strawberries, chopped

STORING

These muffins will keep in an airtight container for up to 2 days.

FREEZING

To freeze, remove the muffins from their cases and flash freeze on a tray or plate for 1 hour until hard. Transfer to a freezer bag or container and freeze for 3 months.

Defrost at room temperature in 3 hours.

METHOD

1. Preheat the oven to 200°C/180°C Fan/ Gas Mark 6 and line a 12-hole muffin tray with paper or silicone cases.

2. Put the flour and baking powder in a large bowl and combine.

3. Place the butter or coconut oil in a large jug and melt in the microwave.

4. Once melted, add the eggs, cream cheese, milk, honey and vanilla and mix well.

5. Add the wet ingredients to the dry ingredients and stir until combined.

6. Finally, fold in the strawberries.

7. Divide the mixture between the 12 muffin cases. I find it easier to do this using an ice cream scoop.

8. Bake in the oven for 20-22 minutes.

NUT-FREE GRANOLA BARS

| Makes: 12 | Prep time: 5 minutes | Cook time: 20 minutes, plus 1 hour cooling | Equipment: Baking dish, large jug and large mixing bowl |

Delicious chewy granola bars made with oats, cereal and seeds. Completely nut-free and ideal to add to lunch boxes for school or nursery.

INGREDIENTS

100g honey

100g butter

25g brown sugar

50ml water

150g oats

30g puffed rice cereal, like Rice Krispies

30g wholemeal flour

2 tbsp seeds

2 tbsp desiccated coconut

STORING

These bars will keep in the fridge for up to 5 days.

FREEZING

Flash freeze the bars on a tray or plate for 1 hour until hard. Transfer to a freezer bag or container and freeze for up to 3 months.

Defrost at room temperature in 1 hour.

METHOD

1. Preheat the oven to 200°C/180°C Fan/ Gas Mark 6 and line a baking dish with parchment paper. I use a 20cm square baking dish.

2. Put the honey and butter in a large jug and microwave until the ingredients have melted.

3. Add the sugar and water and mix until dissolved.

4. Pour the oats, cereal, wholemeal flour, seeds and coconut into a large bowl and mix well.

5. Add in the wet ingredients and mix again until well combined.

6. Transfer this mixture into the dish and press down well with the back of a spoon to make it as compact as possible.

7. Bake for 20 minutes, then remove the dish from the oven and leave to cool.

8. When cool, put the dish directly into the fridge or freezer for 1 hour to cool completely. This is really important to stop the bars from crumbling when cut.

9. After 1 hour, remove the dish from the fridge or freezer. Lift the parchment paper out of the dish and cut into 12 bars.

BOUNTY ENERGY BITES

On-the-go snacking is made easy with these delicious chocolate coconut energy bites, packed full of nutritious and filling ingredients.

INGREDIENTS

100g oats

100g peanut butter

50g desiccated coconut, plus 15g for coating

2 tbsp honey

1 tbsp cocoa power

50ml milk

1 tsp vanilla extract

METHOD

1. Place all the ingredients (except the extra desiccated coconut for coating) into a large bowl and mix with a spoon.

2. Put the extra desiccated coconut on a plate.

3. Take a small amount of the mixture, roll with your hands into a ball and then coat in the extra desiccated coconut.

4. Repeat with the remaining mixture. You should be able to make 16 energy balls.

5. Refrigerate for 30 minutes to firm up.

STORING

These energy bites will keep in a sealed container in a sealed container in the fridge for up to 5 days.

FREEZING

Freeze the energy bites together in a freezer bag or container for up to 3 months. To defrost leave at room temperature for 1 hour.

POPCORN BARS

Makes: 12 | Prep time: 10 minutes, plus 45 minutes freezing time | Cook time: NA | Equipment: Baking dish, large mixing bowl and large jug |

Kids will absolutely love these chocolate Popcorn Bars. Ideal for a tasty treat after school!

INGREDIENTS

50g popcorn (already popped)

50g cornflakes

100g milk chocolate

100g dark chocolate

50g butter

STORING

These bars need to be kept in the fridge and will last for 4–5 days.

METHOD

1. Line a baking dish with parchment paper. I use a 25 x 21cm dish but any similar size dish is fine.

2. Put the popcorn and cornflakes in a large bowl. Crush with your hands just to break them down a little.

3. Place the milk chocolate, dark chocolate and butter in a bowl and melt in the microwave.

4. Pour the melted mixture into the bowl and mix quickly until everything is well combined.

5. Transfer the mixture into the dish and press down with the back of a spoon to make it as compact as possible.

6. Place the dish in the freezer for 45 minutes and then cut into 12 squares.

APPLE PIE WRAPS

| Makes: 4 | Prep time: 5 minutes | Cook time: 25 minutes | Equipment: Saucepan and baking tray |

These baked apple pies are made with mini tortilla wraps and are a tasty and healthier alternative to deep-fried pies.

INGREDIENTS

3 medium apples

4 tbsp water

1 tbsp honey

½ tsp vanilla extract

¼ tsp cinnamon

4 mini tortilla wraps

to coat:

1 tbsp butter

1 tsp sugar

¼ tsp cinnamon

STORING

These wraps are best served immediately but will keep in the fridge for 24 hours.

FREEZING

Freeze the wraps before cooking. After Step 9 place the wraps on a tray or plate and flash freeze for 1 hour until hard. Transfer to a freezer bag or container and freeze for up to 3 months.

Cook directly from frozen at 200°C/180°C Fan/Gas Mark 6 for 20 minutes.

METHOD

1. Chop the apples into small pieces leaving the skins on.

2. Add them to a saucepan with the water and cook with the lid on for 10–12 minutes.

3. Use a potato masher to mash the apples and soak up any water in the pan.

4. Add the honey, vanilla extract and cinnamon and mix well.

5. Preheat the oven to 200°C/180°C Fan/ Gas Mark 6 and line a baking tray with parchment paper.

6. Divide the mixture between the 4 mini wraps, adding it to the centre.

7. Tuck in the sides of the wrap and roll up tightly.

8. Place the rolled-up wraps on the baking tray.

9. Melt the butter and brush it on top, then sprinkle on the sugar and cinnamon.

10. Bake in the oven for 15 minutes.

11. Allow to cool a little before serving.

BIG BATCH BROWNIE MIX

| Makes: 5 batches | Prep time: 5 minutes | Cook time: 17 minutes | Equipment: Large mixing bowl, large jar and brownie tin |

With this recipe you'll never need to buy a box of pre-made brownie mix again. Mix up your own at home, keep it in a jar and, when the mood takes you, whip up a fresh, warm batch of chocolate brownies in no time at all time!

INGREDIENTS

For the big batch:

625g white sugar

500g plain flour

200g chocolate chips

175g cocoa powder

Per batch:

75g butter

2 eggs

1 tsp vanilla extract

STORING

The brownie mixture will keep for up to 3 months. The cooked brownies will last in a cake tin for up to 3 days.

METHOD

1. Pour the sugar, flour, chocolate chips and cocoa powder into a large bowl and mix well.

2. Transfer to a large jar or other airtight container. The brownie mixture will keep for up to 6 weeks.

3. To make one batch of brownies, preheat the oven to 200°C/180°C Fan/Gas Mark 6 and line a brownie tin (about 25 x 22cm) with parchment paper.

4. Take 300g of the brownie mixture and put it in a large bowl.

5. Melt 75g of butter and add that to the mixture, along with the eggs and vanilla.

6. Mix just enough to combine the ingredients and then transfer to the tin.

7. Bake for 15–17 minutes.

8. Allow to cool for a few minutes before cutting into 9 brownies.

FRUIT & VEG FRIDGE PACKS

| Prep time: 10 minutes | Equipment: Glass or plastic containers |

For me, having easy and instant access to fresh fruit and veg is the key to my kids eating healthy snacks throughout the day. Have these packs of ready-prepped veg like carrots, cucumber and peppers and fruit like berries, mango and grapes washed, cut and ready to eat straight from the fridge.

INGREDIENTS

carrots

celery

cucumber

peppers

tomatoes

grapes

berries such as strawberries, blueberries and raspberries

tropical fruit such as pineapple, mango and melon

STORING

Store all the containers in the fridge.

The carrots and celery will last for 3 days. Change the water daily.

The cucumber and peppers will last for 2 days.

The tomatoes will last for 2–3 days.

The fruit will all last 3 days.

METHOD

1. Prep the vegetables first by washing them.

2. Peel and cut the carrots into batons. Cut the celery and cucumber into a similar size and slice the peppers.

3. Place the carrots and celery in a pot or jar and cover with water.

4. Place the cucumber and pepper in a container lined with a damp piece of kitchen paper.

5. Cut the tomatoes in half and place in another container. This one doesn't need kitchen paper.

6. Next, prep the fruit. Wash the berries but keep them whole and place in a container.

7. Prep the tropical fruit by peeling and cutting into bite-sized pieces and placing in another container.

8. Cut the grapes in half and put into another container.

CHOCOLATE ORANGE BROWNIE COOKIES

Delicious double chocolate cookies, crisp on the outside but soft in the middle.

INGREDIENTS

125g unsalted butter, softened

75g light brown sugar

1 egg

grated zest and juice of 1 orange

120g plain flour

120g oats

1 tbsp cocoa powder

½ tsp bicarbonate of soda

50g chocolate chips

STORING

These cookies will keep in an airtight tin for up to 3 days.

FREEZING

Wrap the cookies individually in parchment paper and place in a freezer bag or container for up to 3 months. To defrost, remove from the freezer and defrost for 3 hours at room temperature.

METHOD

1. Preheat the oven to 200°C/180°C Fan/ Gas Mark 6 and line 2 baking trays with parchment paper.

2. Put the softened butter and sugar in a bowl and, using an electric mixer, mix until the ingredients are combined.

3. Add the egg along with the zest and juice of the orange and mix again.

4. Add the flour, oats, cocoa powder and bicarbonate of soda and combine.

5. Finally, stir in the chocolate chips.

6. Divide the mixture into 12 and use your hands to mould into a cookie shape, placing 6 cookies on each tray.

7. Bake in the oven for 15 minutes. Leave the cookies to cool on the tray for a few minutes. This is important to stop them falling apart. Then transfer onto a wire rack to cool completely.

INDEX

First published in the UK by Lagom
An imprint of Bonnier Books UK
Wimpole Street, London, W1G 9RE
Owned by Bonnier Books
Sveavägen 56, Stockholm, Sweden

Hardback – 9781788703598
eBook – 9781788703604

A CIP catalogue of this book is available from the British Library.

Designed by Envy Design
Printed and bound in Poland

1 3 5 7 9 10 8 6 4 2

Lagom is an imprint of Bonnier Books UK
www.bonnierbooks.co.uk

ACKNOWLEDGEMENTS

My first thank you has to be my wonderful audience and followers. From day one you have supported me more than you probably realise. Your messages and comments inspire me daily and have made the My Fussy Eater online family what it is today.

A huge thank you to the team at Bonnier for bringing this book to life. In particular, my brilliant editor Beth for being the biggest cheerleader for this book from the very start. And of course the incredibly talented people at Bonnier who have worked so hard on the copyediting, proof-reading, design, production, marketing, publicity and sales. Thank you to every one of you.

I think everyone can agree just how beautiful the photographs are in this book. To Ella, the photographer, thank you so much. Your talent astounds me. And to food stylist Laura and her assistant Harriet, a massive thank you also. You worked so hard to bring the food to life and I am so grateful. And a big thank you to Amy for the beautiful photos of myself and the children.

To my agent Sarah, thank you for being there for me always. I appreciate your support and advice so much.

Thank you to my family and friends for your continuous encouragement and support. And to my two mini critics at home who are never afraid to let me know when a recipe is not so good!

And to everyone who buys this book... Thank you. I hope it makes your life just a little bit easier in the kitchen.

Editor: Beth Eynon

Photographer: Ella Miller

Food stylist: Laura Fyfe

Food stylist assistant: Harriet Gaffer

Copy-editor: Nicky Jeanes

Proof-reader: Grace Paul

Text designer: Graeme Andrew

Cover designer: Lucy Sykes-Thompson

Cover direction: Emily Rough

Production manager: Alex May